Electronic Organ Servicing Guide

by

Robert G. Middleton

 HOWARD W. SAMS & CO., INC.
THE BOBBS-MERRILL CO., INC.
INDIANAPOLIS · KANSAS CITY · NEW YORK

FIRST EDITION

FIRST PRINTING—1971

International Standard Book Number: 0-672-20826-1
Library of Congress Catalog Card Number: 70-143037

Preface

Organ servicing is an area in which a competent technician can charge what he is worth, and not have the customer raise an eyebrow. It is also an area that tends to "scare" the uninitiated, because an electronic organ is a unique type of audio system. The neophyte assumes that he is at a serious disadvantage if he cannot read music and play an organ. Although it is sometimes helpful to know the fundamentals of musicianship, it is far more important to understand electric and electronic circuitry, principles of ac circuit action, and electronic instrument applications. As a matter of fact, most organ technicians have the traditional "tin ear."

Although an electronic organ appears to be very complicated, this is primarily due to the fact that a certain configuration may be repeated dozens of times, either in identical form, or with progressive changes in component values. An organ is basically simpler than a color-TV receiver. Only audio frequencies are utilized, and there are fewer circuit interactions than in television systems. Because of the repetition in configurations, organ service data appears to be quite voluminous. If the block diagram for an organ is inspected, however, the comparative simplicity of the design plan becomes evident. If the technician has had previous experience in high-fidelity servicing, he will make rapid progress in electronic-organ analysis.

The first chapter discusses general principles and provides a preview of organ circuit action. A system analysis is presented, to provide general perspective. Next, preventive maintenance and evaluation are explained. As in television service, it often happens that tube replacement or contact cleaning is all that is required. Various adjustments and minor repairs also fall into this general category. For example, the organ technician may be called upon to balance the sound levels, or to replace a damaged key. Tone-generator troubleshooting is covered in the fourth chapter. Basically, a tone generator is a single-frequency audio oscillator. This chapter concludes with a review of tuning techniques.

Keying system troubles are explained in the fifth chapter. System design can be categorized into mechanical and electronic systems. That is, the older models of organs in service employ mechanical keyswitches exclusively, whereas the modern trend is to electronic switching with semiconductor devices. However, the initiating key action is still mechanical. Trouble symptoms are often straightforward, although some analysis of the block diagram and schematics will be required in other cases. Voicing troubles are analyzed in the sixth chapter, with stress on filter action inasmuch as most organs use filter networks as waveshapers. Some electronic switching actions are also found in certain voicing sections.

Special voicing facilities, such as piano-harpsichord, glockenspiel, and related functions are covered in the seventh chapter. Although these voicing sections are less commonly encountered, the technician in general practice will find these functions occasionally. Amplifier servicing is discussed next; amplifiers in electronic organs or tone cabinets are found to be quite similar to those employed in high-fidelity systems. However, the power supplies that are used tend to be comparatively sophisticated, and a separate chapter is devoted to this topic.

The final portion of the book includes a technical reference section, and a comprehensive glossary. It is suggested that the glossary be consulted by the apprentice technician whenever doubt arises concerning the definition of a term. In conclusion, it is the author's sincerest belief and hope that the organ servicing information presented in this book will "unscare" many electronic technicians, and open up an unusually profitable field of activity to them.

ROBERT G. MIDDLETON

Contents

CHAPTER 6

CHAPTER 7

CHAPTER 8

CHAPTER 9

Chapter 1

General Principles

Electronic organ operation—producing characteristic musical tones by means of electronic oscillators or equivalent tone sources, mixers, waveshaping circuits, amplifiers, and loudspeakers—is based on principles of circuit action that are well known to professional technicians. The "inside story" of an electronic organ appears complicated to the technician apprentice because of the comparatively large number of circuits, and because the relations among the various circuit sections may not be obvious. Some electronic organs are more complex than others; for example, Fig. 1-1 illustrates an instrument that has only one keyboard (manual), and Fig. 1-2 shows a typical two-manual organ. A three-manual "church" organ is seen in Fig. 1-3, and a three-manual "theater" organ is shown in Fig. 1-4.

Terminology in electronic-organ art and science has been influenced by musicology as well as by audio and electronic engineering. The purpose of this chapter is to briefly familiarize the reader with the more basic electronic-organ principles, and to explain some of the technical terminology. In the great majority of electronic-organ designs, the professional technician stresses the five following sections:

1. Tone generators.
2. Keying system.
3. Voicing section.
4. Audio amplifier.
5. Speaker.

Electronic-organ design varies considerably, and is still in a gradual developmental process. Some form of electronic tone generator is generally used, although we will encounter a few electromechanical tone generators. An occasional electrostatic tone generator might still be in use. Electronic tone generators are familiar arrangements that employ transistors, tubes, or neon bulbs. The basic electromechanical tone generator uses a mechanically driven ferromagnetic tone wheel that varies the strength of a magnetic field through a pickup coil, thereby inducing an ac voltage in the coil. Specialized mechanical tone generators will also be found, such as the metal-bar *glockenspiel* in which certain tones are generated by striking metallic bars, with subsequent amplification of the audio tone. An electrostatic tone generator utilizes a mechanically driven dielectric disc that varies the electrostatic field between a pair of capacitor plates, thereby producing an ac voltage variation between the plates.

Two chief types of keying systems are employed: One design switches circuits that carry audio-frequency currents; the other design switches circuits that carry direct current. The tone generators in some organs operate continuously; in turn, audio-frequency currents must be keyed. In direct keying, this is accomplished by contacts carried by the individual keys. However, in gated keying, diodes or other forms of electronic switches operate between the key contacts and the tone generators; key contacts switch dc circuits in this arrangement. In other designs, the tone generators or oscillators operate only when corresponding keys are depressed; dc circuits are switched by the key contacts. In any case, we state that the tone generator *speaks* when the corresponding key is depressed. A *cipher* is a trouble symptom that refers to a note that plays when it should not.

Fig. 1-1. Orcoa *Concert* chord organ.

Voicing occurs when a tone generator speaks; that is, voicing denotes the sounding of an organ note (or more than one note) with a characteristic tone color or quality. Tone color is also called timbre; it refers chiefly to the harmonic or overtone structure of a tonal waveform. However, there are important secondary factors involved in timbre, as will be explained. Although voicing is a very extensive topic,

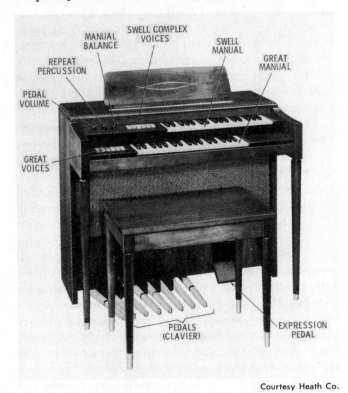

Courtesy Heath Co.

Fig. 1-2. Typical two-manual electronic organ.

Courtesy Rodgers Organ Co.

Fig. 1-3. A three-manual "church" organ.

we will find that three basic designs are of concern to us. First, the required waveform may be produced in a single operation without supplementary devices or circuits; glockenspiel tones produced by striking metal bars are an example of this design. Second, the required waveform may be *synthesized* by mixing suitable combinations of sine waves in various frequency and amplitude relations. Third, the required waveform may be produced by *formants*, which are suitable filter devices that change a reference waveform (such as a square wave) into a musical-tone waveform.

Ohm's law of acoustics, first stated in 1843, reads "Every simple harmonic motion of air is perceived by the ear as a simple tone; all others are resolved by the ear into a series of simple tones of different periods." Although this law is practically true for weak sounds, timbre also depends upon loudness inasmuch as the ear is a nonlinear system. For example, a familiar violin tone becomes "unnatural" if the loudness level is increased 20 phons or more from the normal level. (A phon is equal to a dB at 1 kHz, but becomes progressively unequal at other frequencies.) Again, timbre depends upon pitch (fundamental frequency) as well as upon waveform. For example, if a tape recording of a violin note is played at slow or fast speeds, the violin timbre disappears, although the actual waveform has remained unchanged. Thus, voicing entails art as well as science.

Courtesy Rodgers Organ Co.

Fig. 1-4. A three-manual "theater" organ.

Musicians describe organ voices as reedy, brilliant, mellow, brassy, etc. A *diapason* voice is the tone quality or timbre normally associated with a pipe organ. All electronic organs provide a diapason voice, in addition to others that may be included for special effects. There are other technical considerations concerning timbre, in addition to those that have been noted. These characteristics will be discussed subsequently. From the standpoint of trouble symptoms, distortion is defined somewhat differently in electronic-organ and high-fidelity technology. That is, distortion in organ voicing denotes chiefly a departure from a reference complex waveform. On the other hand, distortion in a hi-fi reproduction denotes a modification of a sine waveform, or of a two-tone sine waveform. Room acoustics may affect the timbre of some sounds, so the inexperienced person may tend to confuse tone distortion with poor room acoustics.

Although amplifier design is comparatively standardized, there are appreciable differences among organ amplifier systems. For example, we may encounter a timbre switch, which modifies the frequency response of an amplifier by switching various RC networks into or out of the tone channel. A single amplifier may be used, or a separate preamplifier may drive one or more power amplifiers. An organ may employ a single 100-watt amplifier, for example, whereas another organ may use three 15-watt amplifiers. When more than one speaker cabinet (tone cabinet) is used, each cabinet may contain an individual amplifier. High-fidelity characteristics do not enter into organ-amplifier design; that is, an organ amplifier serves to *produce* musical tones, whereas a hi-fi amplifier serves to *reproduce* musical tones.

Similarly, organ speakers often differ considerably from hi-fi speakers, since their function is to produce musical tones. An organ speaker is usually designed for operation with a particular organ amplifier. Many speaker designs are in use; some radiate sound through a grille facing the listener, while others radiate sound from a space separating the speaker (or the back of the organ) from the wall of the room. Baffling is usually much different in an organ speaker, compared with a hi-fi speaker. Auxiliary devices may also be employed by organ designers. For example, Allen organs obtain a vibrato effect in voicing by means of a rotating speaker assembly. Each speaker in the assembly is connected to an amplifier output that serves a particular section or voice of the organ. Cone radiators are widely used; exponential horns may be found in elaborate installations.

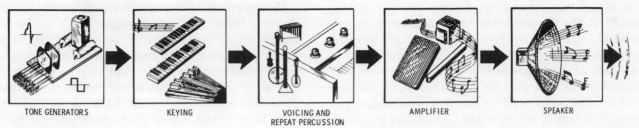

TONE GENERATORS   KEYING   VOICING AND REPEAT PERCUSSION   AMPLIFIER   SPEAKER

Courtesy Heath Co.

Fig. 1-5. The five basic sections used in many modern organs.

SURVEY OF SECTIONS

The majority of modern electronic organs utilize the formant method for producing various voices. Five basic sections are entailed, as shown in Fig. 1-5. We will find that an appreciable number of organs using the synthesis method of tone generation are also in use. In a simplified representation, five basic sections are entailed, as shown in Fig. 1-6. The technical distinction between the formant and the synthesis methods is that the former operates on the basis of waveshaping circuits, whereas the latter builds up tonal waveforms from their fundamental and harmonic components (pitch and overtone components). In the synthesis method, the bass tones may be produced by a specialized electromechanical generator with a rotating ferromagnetic tone wheel that has specially shaped teeth. The bass tone is generated directly, and a complex waveform is obtained without mixing a number of sine waves.

Most modern electronic organs use solid-state oscillators, as shown in Fig. 1-7. It is common design practice to provide one set of master oscillators for the top octave of the organ, and to generate the notes for the lower octaves by means of frequency dividers. Bistable multivibrators are widely used for frequency division, as indicated in Fig. 1-8. Thus, a frequency divider is a tone generator, although it is

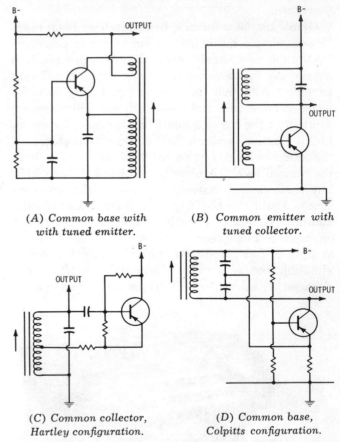

(A) Common base with with tuned emitter.

(B) Common emitter with tuned collector.

(C) Common collector, Hartley configuration.

(D) Common base, Colpitts configuration.

Fig. 1-7. Basic transistor oscillators used in electronic organs.

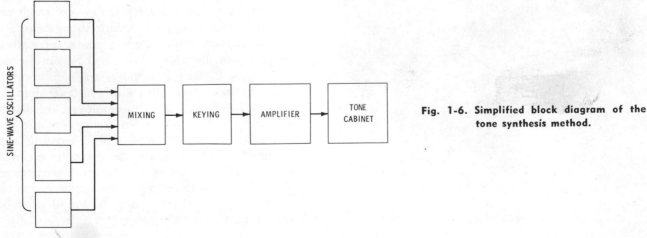

Fig. 1-6. Simplified block diagram of the tone synthesis method.

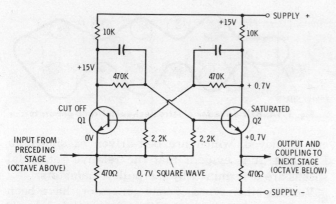

Fig. 1-8. Typical bistable multivibrator configuration used for two-to-one frequency division.

not a master generator. Blocking oscillators (Fig. 1-9) are in extensive use as master oscillators. A blocking oscillator can also serve as a frequency divider, when triggered by a sync signal from a preceding oscillator. Fig. 1-10 shows a tube-type master blocking oscillator, followed by five frequency-divider blocking oscillators. Each divider is a 2-to-1 configuration; thus, the output from V3B has 1/32 the operating frequency of V1A.

Neon-bulb master oscillators are also utilized; Fig. 1-11 shows the basic configuration. This is a single-tube relaxation oscillator. Neon bulbs are also used for frequency division, as shown in Fig. 1-12. Pairs of series-connected neon bulbs are used in a relaxation-oscillator configuration. By applying the sync voltage between a pair of bulbs, more reliable triggering is obtained than if a single-bulb configuration were used. The reason for this is that the entire trigger pulse must flow through the neon bulbs—that is, the trigger circuit is not shunted by any resistive or capacitive branch circuits.

The plan of an electromagnetic tone generator is shown in Fig. 1-13. Tone wheels are driven by a synchronous motor so that the rotational speed is

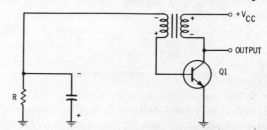

Fig. 1-9. Transistor blocking oscillator.

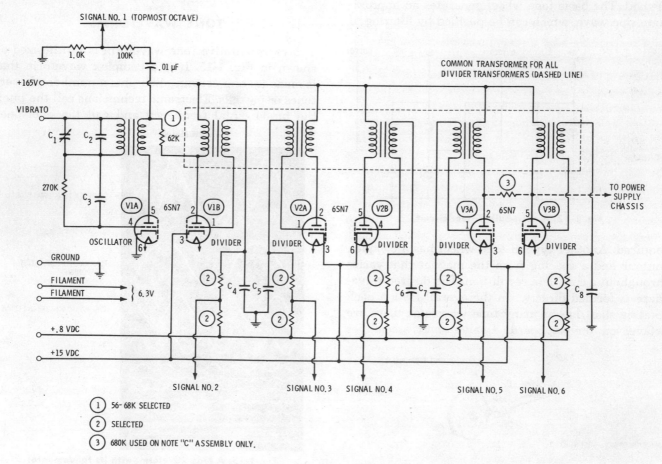

① 56-68K SELECTED

② SELECTED

③ 680K USED ON NOTE "C" ASSEMBLY ONLY.

Fig. 1-10. Tube-type master blocking oscillator, followed by frequency-divider blocking oscillators.

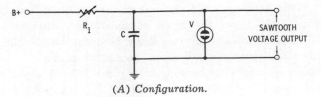

(A) Configuration.

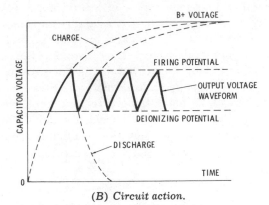

(B) Circuit action.

Fig. 1-11. Neon-bulb oscillator.

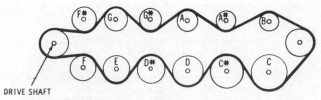

Fig. 1-14. Belt drive for electromechanical tone generator.

unvarying. Each tone wheel is a steel disc, with a typical contour as shown in the diagram. Resulting variations in the magnetic field induce a voltage in the coil. The basic tone wheel generates an approximate sine wave, which can be purified by filtering, if

are employed, which are belt-driven as shown in Fig. 1-14. It is evident that the relative rotational speeds are determined by the pulley diameters.

Various other types of tone generators have been manufactured in the past, although the technician is not very likely to encounter them. The Compton electrostatic tone generator was previously mentioned. The Welte photoelectric tone wheel featured a rotating transparent disc, with 18 concentric "sound tracks" produced by photographic methods. A light beam passing through the disc was modulated and was changed into an electrical output by a photocell. Vibrating reeds and strings have also been used in conjunction with electromagnetic or electrostatic pickups, in addition to the metallic-bar tone generator noted previously.

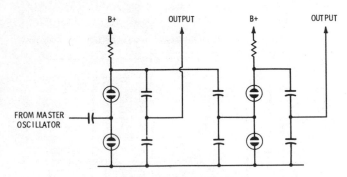

Fig. 1-12. A neon-bulb divider circuit.

required. Another type of tone wheel has a complex contour and a spacing from the magnet that varies throughout a complete revolution. The desired waveshape is formed directly. In the overall layout, each rotating shaft has as many tone wheels as there are octaves on the keyboard. Twelve shaft assemblies

TONE WAVEFORMS

A representative tone waveform is synthesized as shown in Fig. 1-15. It is a complex waveform that is made up of a certain pitch plus a number of overtones or partials. Electronic technicians call the pitch the fundamental frequency and call the overtones

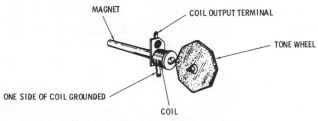

Fig. 1-13. Plan of an electromagnetic tone generator.

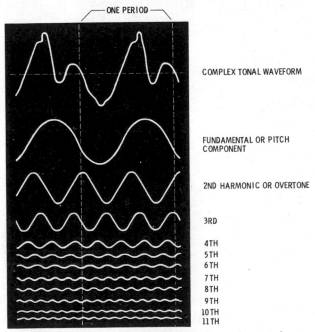

Fig. 1-15. A tone waveform, with its fundamental and harmonics.

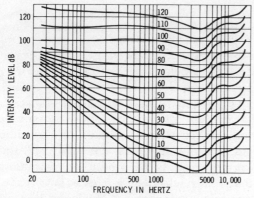

Fig. 1-16. Loudness-level contours (Fletcher & Munson curves).

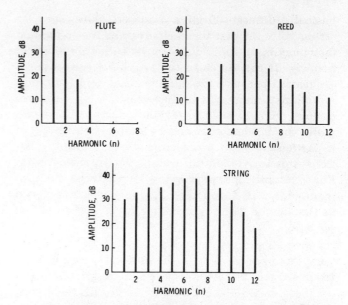

Fig. 1-18. Composition of flute, reed, and string organ voices.

harmonic frequencies. The basic organ tones (voices) have more or less complex waveforms in which all the frequencies in a tone are harmonically related. Each voice has its characteristic harmonic composition that gives the voice its particular tone color or quality (timbre). If the relative phases of the harmonics are changed, the timbre remains unchanged although the waveshape is altered. In other words, the ear responds to the individual harmonics, rather than to the envelope of the complex waveform.

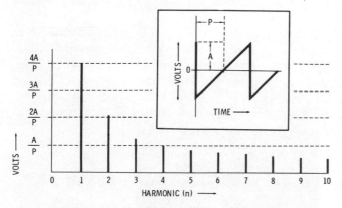

Fig. 1-17. Composition of a sawtooth waveform.

The fact that loudness tends to affect timbre was noted previously. As the loudness is decreased, the low frequencies in a tone tend to disappear, as shown in Fig. 1-16. Therefore, the better organs are designed to compensate for this effect. Well-known waveforms such as a sawtooth wave have a fundamental that is stronger than any of the harmonics, and the harmonics decrease in amplitude progressively, as seen in Fig. 1-17. However, these relations may or may not be true for an organ-voice waveform. With reference to Fig. 1-18, observe that a flute voice does have a composition in the same basic category as a sawtooth waveform. On the other hand, a reed voice has a composition in which the fourth

and fifth harmonics are the strongest components. The string voice also falls into this general category, and the eighth harmonic is the strongest component in this example.

Note that the voices shown in Fig. 1-18 have both even and odd harmonics. A sawtooth waveform also has both even and odd harmonics (Fig. 1-17). Therefore, when a sawtooth is passed through suitable filters, a flute, reed, or string voice can be formed.

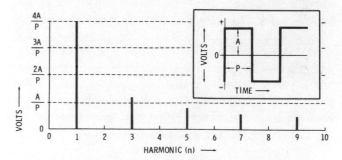

Fig. 1-19. A square wave has odd harmonics only.

The same formant process can be used to produce the diapason (pipe-organ) voice, insofar as an open-pipe voice is concerned. On the other hand, a stopped-pipe diapason voice has a waveform composed of a fundamental and odd harmonics only. Therefore, the sawtooth waveform cannot be employed, and some other waveform that has odd harmonics only must be provided. The square wave (Fig. 1-19) is commonly used to form voices that are composed of odd harmonics only.

An ensemble denotes the performance together of all the instruments of an orchestra, or of all the voices in a chorus. The corresponding waveform is basically different from a diapason, flute, reed, or string voice, in that the ear perceives the individual instruments or individual voices sounding simultaneously. It can do so in the case of a conventional orchestra, because the fundamental tones of individual instruments do not have *exactly* the same frequency, nor *exactly* the same phases. Therefore, while the fundamental and harmonic frequencies of a particular organ voice have exact multiple relations, this is avoided in forming the separate voices. For example, the reed voice is produced in such manner that its fundamental frequency is not locked to that of the string voice and has a slight random variation.

Since it is comparatively difficult to reproduce very low bass tones with the speakers used in electronic organ installations, designers often employ synthetic bass for the lowest tones. In this technique, the fundamental is not generated, and the lower-order harmonics are produced at an increased amplitude. The result is that these harmonics beat together to produce a difference frequency which is that of the missing fundamental. Thereby, the ear is deceived into believing that the fundamental frequency is present. It is the inherent nonlinearity of ear response that makes this technique possible.

Registration is a term that describes the list of stops on the console; the stops are switches that control the various voices that are available. With reference to Fig. 1-2, the stops (also called tabs) are switches for the "Swell complex voices" and the "Great voices." Technicians sometimes apply the term "stops" to the pedal-volume, repeat percussion, and manual balance controls, and apply the term "tabs" to the Swell complex voice and Great voice controls. Vibrato is also an aspect of voicing, rather than of tone generation. This and associated topics are discussed in detail subsequently.

KEYING

The keying circuits are actuated by the manual keys and the clavier pedals (see Fig. 1-2). If the tone generators are blocking oscillators, the key switches ordinarily close associated resistance branches in the RC frequency-determining circuit, as shown in Fig. 1-20. Keying circuits are designed to avoid undesirable "plops" or "clicks" when a circuit is opened or closed. Various methods are used, but the end result in any case is to produce a comparatively gradual rise (attack) and a comparatively gradual decay in normal operation. However, the keying characteristic is not the same for various voices; for example, the string voice requires rapid attack and slow decay, whereas the diapason voice requires slow attack and slow decay. In any keying system, no spurious transients are audible when the circuits are opened or closed in normal operation.

Keying circuits for tone generators that operate continuously are necessarily different from those for tone generators that are switched into and out of oscillation. When audio-frequency currents are keyed, a gradual-contact arrangement may be employed, as exemplified in Fig. 1-21. This is a basic method of avoiding an "explosive" attack when a

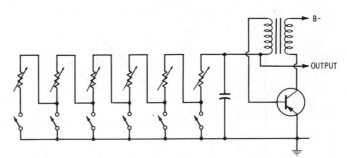

Fig. 1-20. Keying arrangement for a blocking-oscillator tone generator.

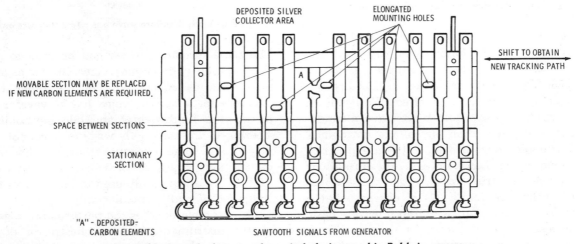

Fig. 1-21. A gradual-contact keyswitch design used in Baldwin organs.

note is sounded. That is, when a key is depressed, the audio current through the contact assembly is given a gradually increasing amplitude, with the current reaching its maximum level shortly before the end of the key motion. Note that when a key is depressed, a deposited-carbon resistive element (A) is gradually keyed out of the circuit. Then, near the end of travel, the keyswitch is completely closed by the deposited-silver surface. When trouble symptoms such as scratchy action, or transient clicks or pops occur, dust particles or other foreign matter is likely to be found on the contacts. We also suspect contact defects when a note is dead; conductive particles can cause cipher symptoms.

Key dip is the total up-and-down travel of a white key. It is normally between 5/16 and 3/8 inch, measured at the end of the key. The term *key leveling* refers to the horizontal plane in which the keys normally rest. Both dip and level are adjustable in most organs. Keyswitch tension denotes the spring pressure that is exerted against downward motion of a key. This force is approximately three ounces in normal operation, and is usually adjustable. When adjusting screws are not provided, flat metal strips and brackets are customarily employed in the assembly, which may be bent slightly as required to obtain normal key action. Fig. 1-22 shows a simple key arrangement. A key may actuate a single pair of contacts, as in Fig. 1-20, or, in other designs it may actuate a number of contacts.

When an organ has two keyboards, the top unit is called the Swell, Solo, or upper manual. The unit below is called the Great, Accompaniment, or lower manual. If three keyboards are provided, the lowermost unit is called the Choir manual. A very elaborate organ may have four or five manuals, and two pedal divisions (claviers). The stop-keys, or tabs, also called stop tablets or stops (Fig. 1-23), are switches that operate in association with the manuals to obtain various tone effects. A coupler is a stop tablet that permits the playing of tones on one manual with the keys of another manual, or the simultaneous sounding of octavely related tones on the same manual.

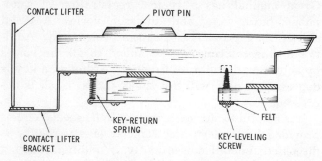

Fig. 1-22. Simple key arrangement.

VOICING AND RELATED FUNCTIONS

In a typical organ, twelve tone generators are keyed. Each tone generator produces the waveforms for one particular note in each octave. For example, a generator that produces a C note is called "tone

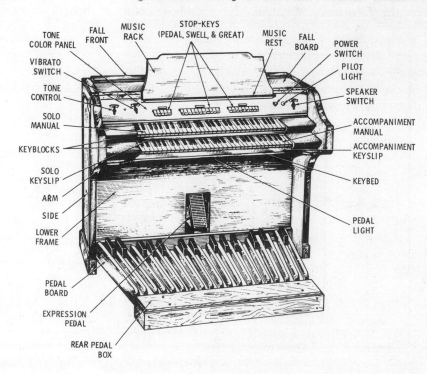

Fig. 1-23. Baldwin console Model 5.

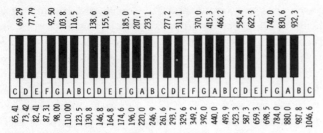

Fig. 1-24. The tone frequency is doubled on successive octaves.

generator C"—it is the source of the tones for all C keys on the manuals and clavier. With reference to Fig. 1-24, a 1046.6-Hz C note can be processed by a 2-to-1 frequency divider to obtain a 523.3-Hz C note. From the keyswitches, the tone signals are fed to the voicing section (see Fig. 1-25). These voicing circuits are controlled by the tabs; when a tab is actuated, the tone color or timbre is changed. When one octave of tone generators is utilized, followed by frequency dividers, the formant method is employed to produce the various voices. Formant circuits are filter networks; for example, typical filter configurations for developing flute, reed, and string voices from a sawtooth wave are shown in Fig. 1-26.

An organ voice does not have exactly the same timbre as the instrument that its name denotes. Although electronic organs have been designed that employ recorded sound tracks to produce exact instrumental timbres, this design has been abandoned, and modern electronic organs are considered to be a particular class of musical instrument. Fig. 1-27 shows the frequency spectrum for an oboe, compared with the frequency spectrum for the oboe voice of an electronic organ. Vibrato is also an aspect of voicing. It often consists of a variation in pitch at a rate of 5 to 8 Hz. That is, vibrato may entail a frequency modulation of the tone. In other designs, vibrato may be an amplitude modulation, or a combination of fm and a-m.

Percussion is the effect produced by musical instruments in which tones result from plucking or striking strings, as in a piano or guitar. When a percussion voice is automatically repetitive, it is called a repeat-percussion function. It produces a variable strumming characteristic in the tones. As noted previously, the lowest-frequency tones are keyed by the pedals; the volume is also controlled by pedals. The volume control for the entire organ is called the expression pedal. In a typical organ, two 37-note manuals and a 13-note pedal clavier are provided. A Swell manual has a typical registration of trombone, reed, flute, oboe, cornet, and violin voices. A Great manual has a typical registration of saxophone, horn, viola, and diapason vocies. A Pedal clavier may provide a diapason voice only. Additional tone coloring can be added to all the voices by actuating the vibrato function. Although a key is depressed, a note will not speak unless a tab is depressed.

It is helpful to survey briefly various special effects provided by modern electronic organs; circuitry is discussed in detail subsequently. In addition to string voices, other percussion effects include wood-block, bongo, snare-drum, bass-drum, clave, and cymbal

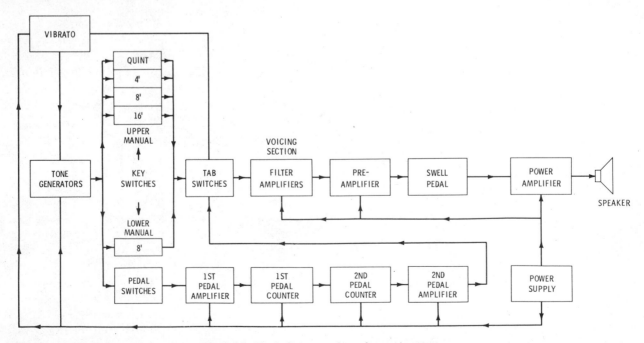

Fig. 1-25. Block diagram of an electronic organ.

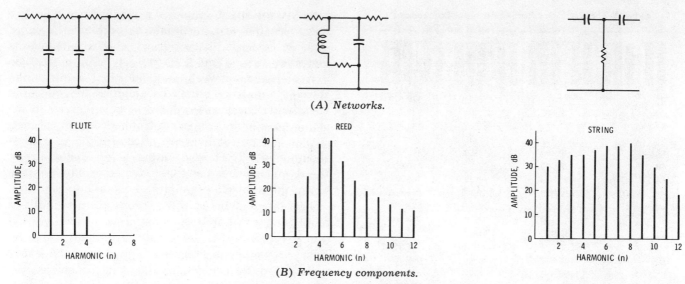

(A) *Networks.*

(B) *Frequency components.*

Fig. 1-26. Typical formant filter configurations.

voices. Cymbal and brush voices are developed from the outputs of noise generators. A snare-drum voice is produced by mixing a pulse-type waveform with noise voltages. Carillon and chimes effects may be provided. Voices characterized by waveforms with fast rise can be processed readily when audio-frequency currents are keyed. When tone generators are keyed off and on, chiff circuits are employed in some designs to obtain fast rise. Chiff effects modify the sound in a characteristic manner, and the timbre is recognizably different from that produced by audio-frequency keying.

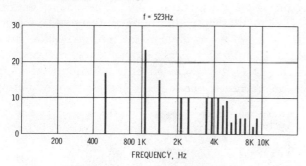

(A) *Frequency spectrum of an oboe.*

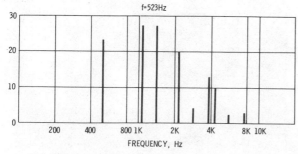

(B) *Frequency spectrum of an oboe organ voice.*

Fig. 1-27. Variation in tonal spectra.

To obtain improved simulation of pipe-organ tones, a whind effect may be provided for the diapason voices. Whind emphasizes certain harmonics in the tone waveform during its rise time; although the fundamental has the greatest amplitude in the steady state, certain harmonics have the greatest amplitude during the transient period when the whind effect is employed. The vox-angelica voice is characterized by a notably refined tone quality. A vox humana tone simulates the human voice and also employs a tremolant in most cases. The wow-wow effect is related to vibrato, but has a slower frequency and greater amplitude variation. A chord is a combination of harmonious tones that are sounded together. On a chord organ, a full chord is played by depressing a single chord button. The choir or chorus effect indicates simultaneous sounding of a number of voices. This may be effected by means of separate oscillators, or by applying vibrato to part of the sound, while reproducing other parts without vibrato. Various other special effects are explained in later chapters.

OSCILLATOR AND NOTE FREQUENCIES

An occasional electronic organ employs a separate oscillator for each note, or a series of tone wheels on individual shafts for each note. However, most organs use master oscillators and frequency dividers. For example, we will often find 12 master oscillators, with two frequency dividers for each master oscillator. With reference to Table 1-1, the master oscillators commonly range in frequency from 523.251 Hz to 1046.502 Hz. All notes with frequencies below this range are obtained by frequency-divider action in

Table 1-1. Master Oscillator and Note Frequencies

Note	Frequency in Hz	Note	Frequency in Hz
C1	65.406	D3	293.665
C#1	69.296	D#3	311.127
D1	73.416	E3	329.628
D#1	77.782	F3	349.228
E1	82.407	F#3	369.994
F1	87.307	G3	391.995
F#1	92.499	G#3	415.305
G1	97.999	A3	440.000
G#1	103.826	A#3	466.164
A1	110.000	B3	493.883
A#1	116.540	C4	523.251
B1	123.470	*C#4	554.365
C2	130.810	*D4	587.330
C#2	138.591	*D#4	622.254
D2	146.832	*E4	659.255
D#2	155.563	*F4	698.456
E2	164.814	*F#4	739.989
F2	174.614	*G4	783.991
F#2	184.997	*G#4	830.609
G2	195.998	*A4	880.000
G#2	207.652	*A#4	932.328
A2	220.000	*B4	987.767
A#2	233.082	*C5	1046.502
B2	246.942		
C3 (Middle)	261.626		
C#3	277.183		

*The last twelve notes are the frequencies at which the twelve master oscillators in the organ operate.

the usual system. In a typical organ, there are 87 keys and pedals, but only 49 note frequencies. This is because the Great manual overlaps the Swell manual, and the Pedal clavier overlaps the Great manual.

Practically all electronic organs employ the equally tempered scale. This means that any one note has the same spacing from its adjoining note as any other note on the manual. That is, each note is approximately 6 percent higher in frequency than its adjoining lower note. Any two notes, spaced by an octave (12 intervals) apart, have a frequency ratio of exactly 2-to-1. It follows that if the output from a tone generator has odd harmonics only (such as a square waveform), a waveform with both even and odd harmonics can be formed by mixing a note with another note that is an octave higher in frequency. The result is to change the square wave into a rectangular wave that has both even and odd harmonics.

ORGAN SPEAKERS

Speakers and tone cabinets used with electronic organs were briefly noted previously. There is considerable variation in tone-cabinet design. The sim-

plest arrangement employs a single large speaker that uses the organ cabinet as a baffle. A large speaker is basic, in order to obtain satisfactory low-frequency output. The majority of organs utilize a woofer and a tweeter; in addition, a mid-range speaker (squawker) may be included. When ample installation space is available, it is preferred to install a tone cabinet separate from the organ cabinet. A pair of tone cabinets are often utilized in a large room or hall. The sound output is less disturbing to the organist when the tone cabinet or cabinets are not in the immediate vicinity of the manuals.

The larger tone cabinets often contain built-in amplifiers, so that less demand is placed on the power capability of the organ output amplifier. As noted previously, baffling is designed from the standpoint of sound projection. Fig. 1-28 illustrates the portion of a typical tone cabinet containing a rotating element. Signals from a built-in amplifier feed a 12-inch speaker in this section of the cabinet. As the sound waves radiate from the speaker through the baffle, the sound energy is deflected by the disc rotating with a velocity of approximately 7 revolutions per second. The inclined disc is driven by a small motor in much the same way as the turntable of a record player.

Radiation from the back of the speaker in Fig. 1-28 is absorbed by the space in the upper section of the cabinet compartment. This back radiation is not permitted to emerge from the tone cabinet, because it would tend to defeat the fluctuation of amplitude produced by the rotating disc. The sound energy that is modulated by the inclined disc emerges from three sides of the compartment through grille openings. From the technical point of view, the rotating disc produces a Doppler effect in addition to the amplitude variation. That is, a frequency-modulation

Fig. 1-28. Inclined rotating disc produces both amplitude variation and a Doppler effect.

Fig. 1-29. Woofer, tweeter, and drone arrangement for organ sound radiation.

effect is produced in addition to an amplitude-modulation effect. The other compartment of the tone cabinet in Fig. 1-28 (not shown in the photo) is comparatively conventional, and houses two 12-inch speakers. These speakers radiate on axes separated by an angle of 45°, so that the acoustic output from one speaker is heard at a slightly different phase from that of the other.

The arrangement illustrated in Fig. 1-29 provides a woofer and a tweeter in a tone cabinet that would represent an infinite baffle, if it were not for the

Fig. 1-30. Gyrophonic speaker assembly used in Allen organs.

drone speaker at top left. That is, the cabinet space is completely enclosed, but back radiation from the woofer at bottom right vibrates the cone of the drone, which operates as a parasitic radiator. This type of speaker is operated facing a wall, with a separation of several inches. Sometimes the speaker assembly is built into the back of the electronic organ. Or, the speaker assembly may be installed separately, facing some other wall of the room. Two or more units may be employed in a large room, and will provide better diapason voices. When one unit is operated, and is built into the back of the organ, the chief advantage is a reduction in distraction to the organist, compared with a front-radiating speaker in the organ.

Still another speaker arrangement is shown in Fig. 1-30. This is called a gyrophonic speaker assembly. It consists of three speakers mounted in a rotating unit and two fixed speakers. Each of the moving speakers serves a separate voice from the organ. When this mechanical vibrato effect is combined with the output from a fixed speaker driven by the same voice signal, an ensemble or choral effect is provided. As in the previous example, the gyrophonic speaker assembly is designed to operate facing a wall at a distance of several inches. When mechanical vibrato is used, it is often called a "theatrical tremolo"; when electronic vibrato is used, it is referred to as simply "vibrato."

TYPICAL SYSTEM ANALYSIS

Because of the wide range of possibilities in electronic-organ design, it is evident that all the sections must operate harmoniously from the systems viewpoint. In this topic, the interactions of the following typical subsystems will be outlined:

1. Tone generators.
2. Distribution board.
3. Swell keyboard.
4. Great keyboard.
5. Pedal chassis, Pedal and low-C divider board.
6. Voicing networks.
7. Amplifier, vibrato network, and power supply.
8. Repeat percussion circuit.

The block diagram in Fig. 1-31 shows the main subsystems with which we are concerned in this example. Since a tone generator is a signal source, it follows that if a tone generator "goes dead," operates off-frequency, produces an incorrect output waveform, or applies a subnormal voltage to the keying section, the operation of the voicing and amplifier sections will be impaired, and the speaker will

19

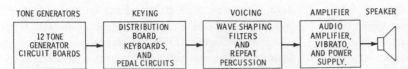

Fig. 1-31. Block diagram of a typical electronic organ.

produce a distorted sound output. With reference to Fig. 1-32, the master oscillator employs a basic Hartley circuit and triggers a frequency divider. In turn, the first frequency divider triggers a second frequency divider. Thus, each tone-generator sub-system provides three frequency sources: the master-oscillator output, the first-divider output, and the second-divider output. Twelve of these tone-generator circuit boards are used in this example. Note that the boards are identical, except for the values of C101, C102, and C103, which establish the frequency of the master oscillator. These divider boards all use the same component values, because a bistable multivibrator (flip-flop) has two stable stages, regardless of the input trigger frequency.

Trouble in the foregoing subsystem can be localized to advantage by means of a scope and dc voltmeter. For example, the normal collector waveform appears as shown in Fig. 1-33. If the waveform is observed to be distorted, we will look for a defective component in the master-oscillator subsection. Dc voltage measurements often suffice to close in on a fault, and continuity or resistance measurements may be helpful. The steep negative-going peak of the waveform shown in Fig. 1-33 serves as a trigger

pulse for the first frequency divider in Fig. 1-32. Note the vibrato-input terminal in Fig. 1-32. When the vibrato tab is actuated, a vibrato input signal with a frequency of approximately 6 Hz is coupled to the base of transistor Q101. In turn, the output from the master oscillator is frequency-modulated at a 6-Hz rate. There is also some amplitude modulation of the master-oscillator output. However, the frequency dividers are only frequency-modulated; a flip-flop cannot be amplitude-modulated by varying the trigger amplitude.

Next, let us consider the operation of the frequency-divider subsections. Fig. 1-34 shows the semisquare output waveform from the first divider. It has a repetition rate that is exactly one-half that of the master-oscillator waveform shown in Fig. 1-33.

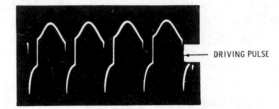

Fig. 1-33. Normal collector waveform for the exemplified tone generator.

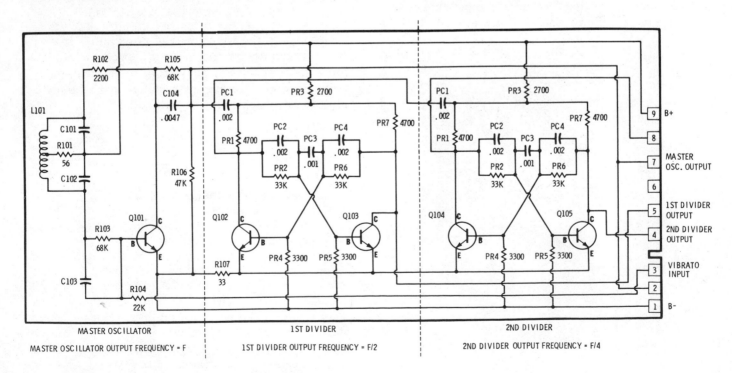

Fig. 1-32. Tone-generator and frequency-divider configuration.

This is the result of the flip-flop operation of Q102 and Q103 in Fig. 1-32. That is, it requires two input trigger pulses to drive the flip-flop through a complete cycle of operation. Similarly, the semisquare output waveform from the second divider (Fig. 1-35) has a repetition rate that is one-half that of the first

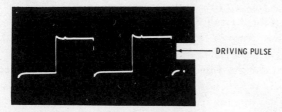

Fig. 1-34. Output waveform from the first frequency divider.

divider output (Fig. 1-34). The twelve tone-generator circuit boards in this example feed their outputs to a distribution board, as seen in Fig. 1-36. The low-C tone generator is also a frequency divider (see Fig. 1-37). This distribution board is more than a central terminal location, in that it also includes packaged electronic circuits (PECs), shown in Fig.

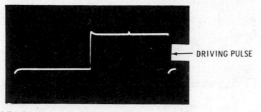

Fig. 1-35. Output waveform from the second frequency divider.

1-38. There is one PEC for each tone generator; each PEC is basically a mixing circuit.

As noted previously, each tone-generator board provides three octaves of output signals for its particular note. That is, one note in the first octave is produced by the master oscillator, a half-frequency note in the next octave is produced by the first frequency divider, and a quarter-frequency note in the following octave is produced by the second frequency divider. Technicians who are adept in waveform analysis will recognize that the waveform in

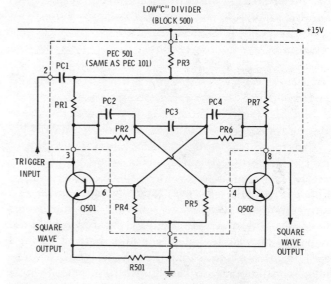

Fig. 1-37. The low-C tone generator is a flip-flop configuration.

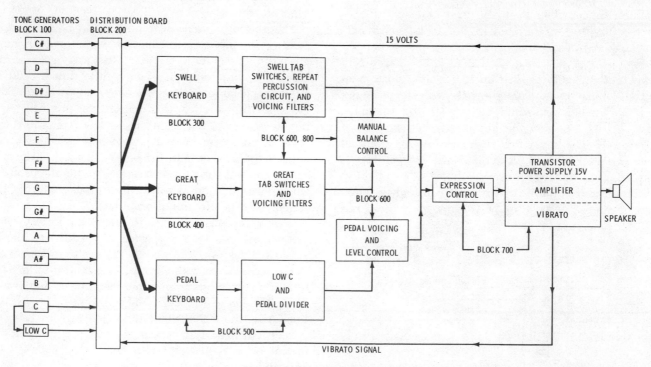

Fig. 1-36. Subsystem flow chart.

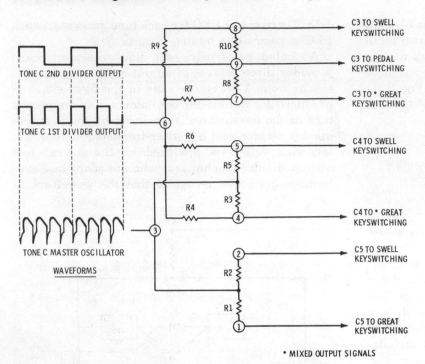

Fig. 1-38. Packaged electronic circuit used on the distribution board.

Fig. 1-33 entails both even and odd harmonics. We know that a square wave contains odd harmonics only. But inasmuch as the PEC boards mix these two waveforms, the sum contains both even and odd harmonics. Note that the input signals are applied continuously to the distribution board—it is the output signals from the distribution board that are keyed (switched) by the organist.

When the outputs from the first and second frequency dividers are mixed in the PEC board networks, a staircase waveform is produced, as shown in Fig. 1-39. A staircase waveform is comparable to a sawtooth waveform, in that it contains both even and odd harmonics. This staircase waveform is fed to a particular keyswitch on one of the manuals. Now, let us consider the keyboard sections shown in Fig. 1-36. The keyswitch circuitry for this example is shown in Fig. 1-40. A typical key mechanism is seen in Fig. 1-41. We observe that the Swell keyswitch section employs three keying branches. Thirteen keys operate on the low-frequency branch, and

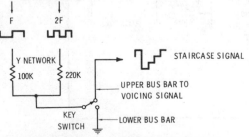

Fig. 1-39. Formation of a staircase signal.

12 keys each operate on the midrange frequency and high-frequency branches. The reason for this division is to restrict the range of frequencies that must be processed by each of the subsequent formant filters. For example, the flute voice is a comparatively pure sine-wave signal. It is easier to process a complex input waveform into a reasonable facsimile of a sine wave if the 12 highest notes can be fed to a separate formant network.

Theoretically, each flute note could be formed by passing its associated complex waveform through an individual low-pass filter. In such a case, the small harmonic content of each flute note would be exactly the same as that of its companion flute notes. However, in practice, this elaboration of circuitry is not necessary. That is, a single low-pass filter can serve a complete octave of notes satisfactorily. Of course, the first note in the octave has a greater harmonic content than the last note. The justification for this approximation of a true flute tone is simply the judgment of professional organists.

With reference to Fig. 1-40, the Pedal keyswitches provide a one-octave extension of the low-frequency range of the Great manual. As seen in Fig. 1-38, Pedal signals are taken from the second divider output, without modification by the mixing networks. Thus, the Pedal source signal is a semisquare wave. Insofar as the Pedal notes indicated in Fig. 1-40 are concerned, it would appear that they duplicate the lowest octave on the Great manual. Actually, we will find that the output signal from the Pedal key-

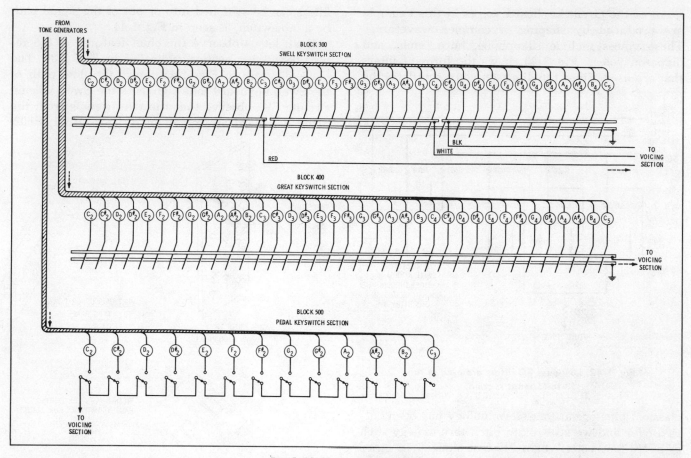

Fig. 1-40. Keyswitch circuitry.

switch section is fed to still another frequency divider. As a result, the notes played by the pedals are placed an octave lower than the lowest notes on the Great manual. This pedal-note frequency divider produces an output square wave; however, the output waveform is mixed with the input waveform to form a staircase wave that is then fed to the pedal voicing filter.

The voicing filters in this example are divided into separate groups for the Swell and the Great keyboard voices, as shown in Fig. 1-36. The Swell keyboard voicing filters are further divided into the flute and the complex groups. Observe in the upper portion of Fig. 1-40 how separate input signals for these two groups are obtained from the three Swell-

keyboard switch sections. Low-pass filters (RC networks) used to form the flute voice signal are shown in Fig. 1-42. Also, branch circuits through R601, R602, and R603 feed the complex waveform signals to other formant circuitry. In this circuitry, trombone, reed, oboe, cornet, and violin voices are formed. This formant circuitry employs suitable combinations of capacitors, resistors, and inductors, to obtain the necessary waveshaping actions. Each formant filter is switched into or out of the signal path by a tab switch. All voices from the Swell keyboard are fed to a manual balance control and through an expression (pedal) volume control as shown in Fig. 1-36. The output signals from the expression control are then amplified and fed to the speaker(s).

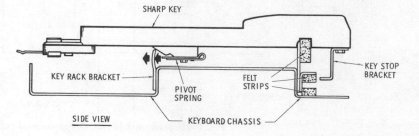

Fig. 1-41. Typical key mechanism.

All of the Great keyboard voices in this example are produced by shaping of complex waveforms. These voices include saxophone, horn, viola, and diapason voices. Fig. 1-43 shows the formant filters that are used. Since the diapason voice simulates the

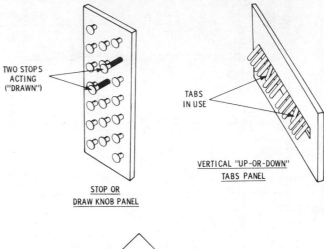

Fig. 1-42. Low-pass RC filters are used in this flute-formant section.

classical pipe-organ tone, terminology has been carried over and we still retain pitch terminology such as a "16-foot voice," or a "16-foot signal." In other words, the frequency of the fundamental tone produced by an organ pipe is a function of its length. For example, a 16-foot signal has a fundamental frequency of 32.5 Hz; an 8-foot signal has a fundamental frequency of 65 Hz. Each of the formant

filters can be switched into or out of the signal path by a tab switch, as seen in Fig. 1-44.

Next, let us observe the chief features of the repeat-percussion section indicated in Fig. 1-36. The block diagram in Fig. 1-45 shows the flow path of the Swell keyboard tone signals to the Swell voicing circuits. We observe that the tone signals from the Swell keyboard are mixed in resistors R601, R602,

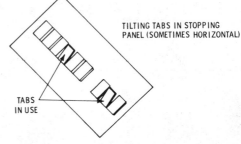

Fig. 1-44. Conventional types of tabs (stops or drawknobs).

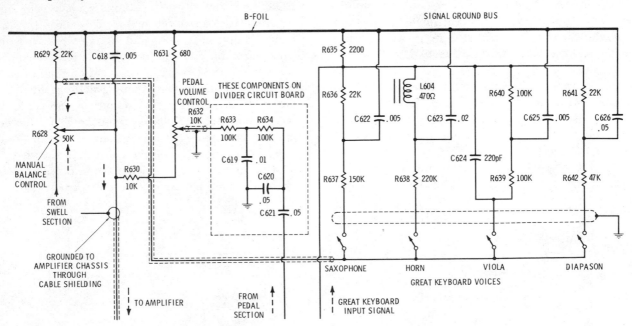

Fig. 1-43. Formants for the Great-manual voices.

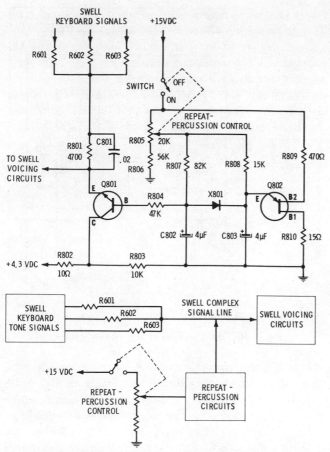

and R603, and are fed to the Swell complex-signal line. These mixed signals feed directly to the voicing circuits when the repeat-percussion switch is off. However, when the switch is turned on, the mixed signals flow into the repeat-percussion circuit, which in turn causes an interruption of the signal at a rate determined by the setting of the repeat-percussion control.

Operation of the repeat-percussion control in Fig. 1-45 starts with the charging of C803 through R808. Capacitor C802 also charges through R807, but at a slower rate. This slower charging rate maintains diode X801 in a nonconducting state. Next, as C802 charges above 4.3 volts, transistor Q801 becomes forward-biased through R804. Transistor conduction effectively switches the signal to ground. When C803 has charged above the firing level of unijunction transistor Q802, C802 and C803 discharge through the emitter and base-1 (B1) junction. If the repeat-percussion control is turned counterclockwise, the voltage applied to R808 decreases. In turn, C803 takes longer to charge, and the oscillation rate slows down. On the other hand, turning the repeat-percussion control clockwise increases the rate of oscillation.

The circuit for the associated organ amplifier is shown in Fig. 1-46. All of the tone signals are applied through the expression (volume) control to the base

Fig. 1-45. Repeat-percussion configuration.

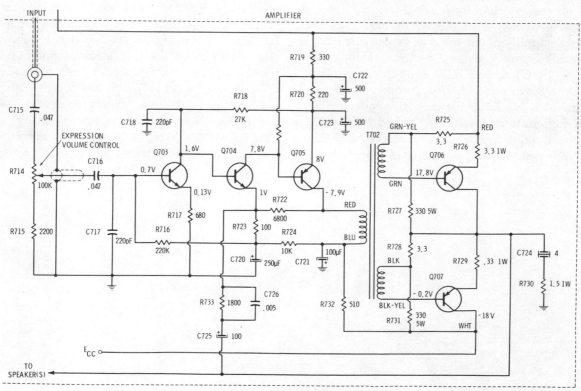

Fig. 1-46. Amplifier configuration.

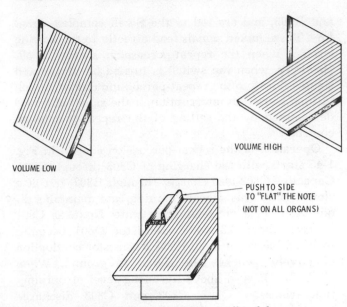

VOLUME HIGH

VOLUME LOW

PUSH TO SIDE
TO "FLAT" THE NOTE
(NOT ON ALL ORGANS)

Fig. 1-47. Functions of the swell pedal.

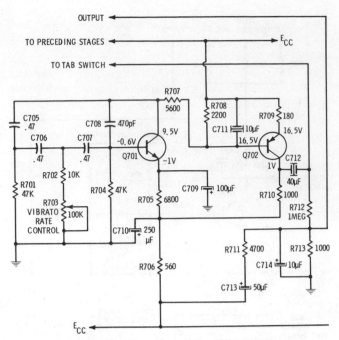

Fig. 1-48. Configuration of the vibrato section.

of the first transistor. This control is also called the Swell pedal, as indicated in Fig. 1-47. In the example of Fig. 1-46, a three-stage dc-coupled amplifier is employed. The output transistors Q706 and Q707 operate in a single-ended push-pull configuration. That is, Q706 is driven by one-half of the secondary on transformer T702, whereas Q707 is driven by the other half of the secondary on T702. Class-B operation is used, and the output transistors conduct alternately on opposite half cycles of the signal.

Negative feedback is employed in Fig. 1-46 to linearize the amplifier and to provide extended flat frequency response. A voltage-feedback loop, consisting of C725, C726, and R733 couples the output signal back to the emitter of Q704. Another feedback loop is provided by R722 between the collector of Q705 and the emitter of Q704. C724 and R730 provide equalization for the inductive component of the speaker voice coil, thereby assisting in maintaining uniform frequency response. A plug is provided for driving a separate speaker, if desired. Note that separate tone cabinets may contain built-in amplifiers—this is a desirable feature whenever substantial demand is made on the output power from the organ.

With reference to Fig. 1-48, the vibrato configuration is basically a 6-Hz oscillator circuit (Q701). A phase-shift feedback network is used, and the exact frequency of oscillation can be adjusted by means of R703. The output signal from Q701 is fed through resistor R707 to the base of vibrato-amplifier transistor Q702. The amplified signal from the collector of Q702 is coupled via C712 to the vibrato tab switch, and thence to the tone-generator section as noted previously. Note that there is a technical distinction between vibrato and tremolo; vibrato is defined as fm, whereas tremolo is defined as a-m.

Chapter 2

Preventive Maintenance
and Evaluation

Preventive maintenance has the purpose of detecting potential trouble conditions and correcting them before organ operation is impaired. Thus, the goal is to keep an organ in optimum operating condition; however, occasional failures or breakdowns will occur in spite of systematic preventive-maintenance procedures. Cleaning procedures are basic, along with a checkout of all functions. In the case of tube-type organs, replacement of weak or otherwise marginal tubes is an important preventive-maintenance procedure. Note that electrical or mechanical failures, such as defective capacitors, damaged switches, burnt-out resistors or printed-circuit conductors, are classified as troubleshooting requirements. Organ tuning is also in the troubleshooting classification. Although there is no sharp dividing line between preventive maintenance and troubleshooting, it is nevertheless helpful to make a general distinction.

BASIC MAINTENANCE

Routine dusting and/or wiping of the manuals with a soft- damp cloth will keep the keys from appearing dull or smudged. If necessary, preliminary cleaning can be done with mild soap on a dampened cloth; however, be careful to avoid trickling of moisture between the keys. Tabs can be similarly dusted or cleaned. Wood surfaces usually require dusting only. Accidental scratches can be made less visible by use of a scratch-stick. Mahogany, walnut, and light tones are commonly available, to match the particular type of wood that is of concern. Deep

scratches or dents can be filled with a crayon-stain filler, and finished by brushing with a suitable coloring liquid. Comparatively elaborate cabinet-repair kits are also available for technicians who wish to do professional cabinet-refinishing jobs. In routine maintenance, consoles and tone cabinets can be polished occasionally with red oil or equivalent furniture polish.

TUBE REPLACEMENT

Weak tubes are the most common cause of subnormal sound output in the older types of organs. Fig. 2-1 illustrates a bank of tubes in a typical instrument. These tubes are contained in the console, and are accessible when the back cover is removed. Again, tubes are often located on amplifier chassis in tone cabinets, as shown in Fig. 2-2. Twin triodes such as the 12AU7 or 6SN7 are in extensive use, although pentodes such as the 6BQ5 or beam-power tubes such as the 6V6 are commonly found in the output stages. Power supplies generally employ 5U4 rectifier tubes. Organ technicians seldom utilize tube testers; instead, it is preferred to test a tube for operation in the circuit of concern.

Let us first consider a simple type of organ with built-in speakers. Fig. 2-3 shows a schematic diagram for a typical amplifier section. If any tube in this section becomes weak, the sound output will be limited, regardless of the voice signal or the manual that is checked. This is a basic example of logical reasoning that can save considerable time that would be wasted in a "shotgun" approach. The service manual for an organ usually provides a tube-layout diagram, as exemplified in Fig. 2-4. If there are no weak tubes in the amplifier section, limited sound output can also be caused by subnormal B+ voltage to the output tubes. Therefore, the rectifier tube in the power supply (usually a 5U4) should also be checked. In case the weak-sound symptom persists, systematic troubleshooting procedures are required, as explained subsequently.

If the console is interconnected with a pair of tone cabinets, and there is subnormal sound output from one of the cabinets, the symptom provides preliminary localization. Some manufacturers recommend installing a complete new set of tubes after a thousand hours of use, whether the sound output appears to be normal or not. The reason for this schedule is that the amplifier tubes often fail gradually, with the result that substandard operation might be occurring for some time before the organist is definitely aware of a trouble symptom. Statistically, it may be noted that tubes tend to be shorter-lived when operated at high power levels. That is, with all other things being equal, power output tubes will require replacement before preamplifier tubes.

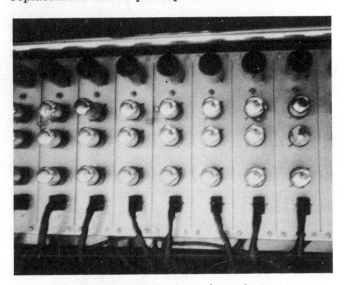

Fig. 2-1. Bank of tubes in an electronic organ.

Technicians who have become experienced in servicing a particular model or brand of organ know immediately which tube to check when an individual key produces subnormal sound output. However, most technicians service more than one type of organ, and it becomes necessary to consult the schematic diagram and service manual for the instrument, to avoid a "shotgun" approach. It is also helpful to have an understanding of the basic functional systems, so that service data can be evaluated rapidly. We may observe in this regard that only a few

organs employ individual oscillators for each note. A block diagram for a typical shared-oscillator system is shown in Fig. 2-5. Note that each tone generator can produce three notes (the first tone generator can produce four notes).

With reference to Fig. 2-5, each tube can be energized by any one of three keys, the three keys being adjacent to each other. For example, one tube will respond when the C, C♯, or D key is depressed. Thus, a choice of three oscillator frequencies is provided by each tone-generator tube. It is evident that if the C♯ key is depressed, the C and D keys will remain "dead" until the C♯ key is released. In other words, conventional oscillators can be operated at only a single frequency at a time. This tone-generator arrangement is practical, because musicians very seldom play two adjacent notes separated by a whole tone or less. Note that the interval from C to D is a whole tone, and that the interval from C to C♯ is a semitone. Sixteen tone-generator tubes are used in the example of Fig. 2-5.

Fig. 2-2. Amplifier chassis in a tone cabinet.

Fig. 2-6 shows the tone-generator circuitry used in this arrangement. A Hartley oscillator is used, and the grid of the 12AU7 is connected to switch D, the highest in the series of three. Note that the cathode bias voltage normally cuts off the oscillator tube via R1. Next, let us suppose that the C switch is closed; in turn, a positive voltage is applied through R5 to the grid of the oscillator tube, thereby starting oscillation. At the same time, capacitor C3 is shunted across C1 to produce the frequency for a C note. C4 operates as a blocking capacitor. We observe that if the C♯ switch should be closed also, then C2 becomes operative, instead of C3, and the oscillator frequency

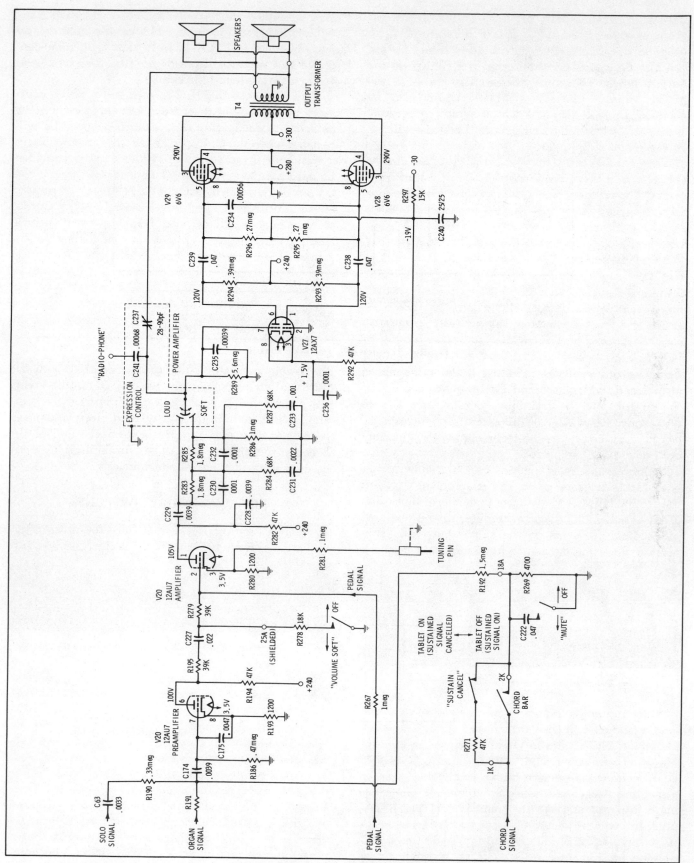

Fig. 2-3. Preamplifier and amplifier circuits.

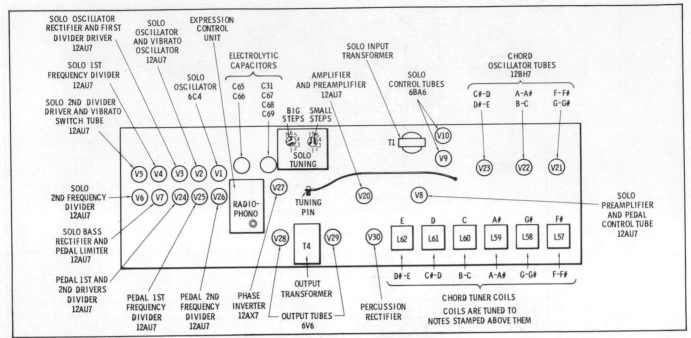

Fig. 2-4. Top view of a generator chassis.

increases one semitone. Finally, if the D switch is also closed, both the C and C♯ branches are out of the circuit, and the oscillator operates at a D-note frequency. Knowledge of this circuit-action response can be very helpful to the technician when "buzzing out" an unfamiliar model.

If the organ service manual does not show a one-note block diagram, as in the example of Fig. 2-7, the technician should evaluate the general block diagram or schematic diagram to determine a one-note block diagram. Thus, if the sound output is sub-normal when the particular key is depressed, check

the 1-note oscillator tube (assuming that both the flute and string voices are weak). Or, if the string voice is normal, check the preamplifier and the post-amplifier tubes. The ability to read electronic-organ schematic diagrams requires experience and study, because the circuit actions are unfamiliar in some cases to general electronic technicians.

KEY AND PEDAL SWITCHES

Various types of keyswitches are found in different organs. Switches can be broadly classified into

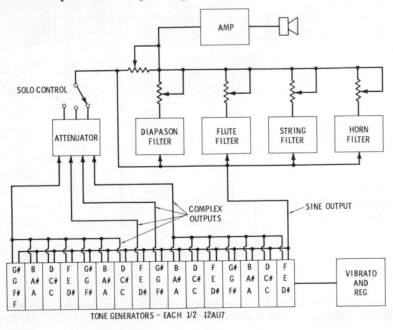

Fig. 2-5. Block diagram of shared-oscillator system.

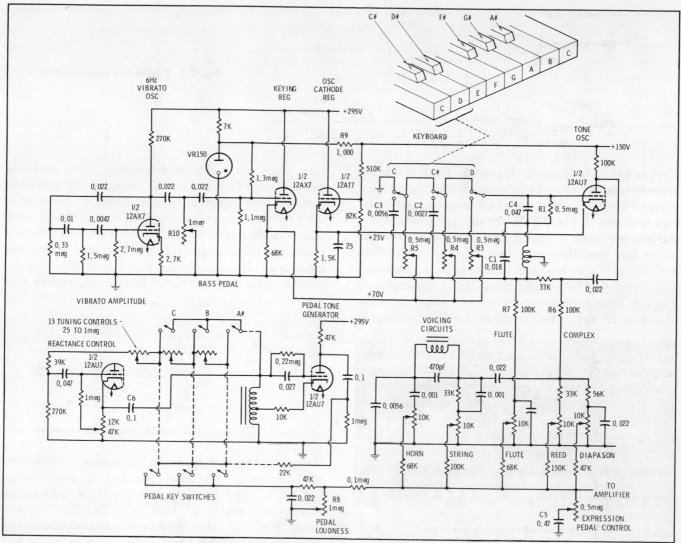

Fig. 2-6. Tone-generator circuitry for a shared-oscillator system.

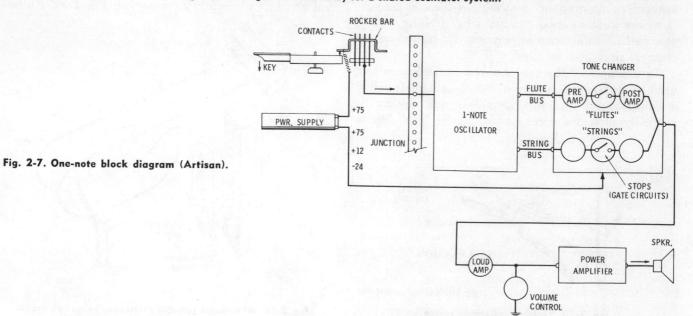

Fig. 2-7. One-note block diagram (Artisan).

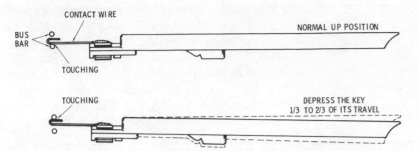

Fig. 2-8. Typical key contact action.

mechanical and electronic types. Mechanical designs are subclassified into the all-or-none and the gradual (resistance) types. A typical all-or-none switch design is shown in Fig. 2-8. When the key is depressed, the contact wire is raised and presses against the upper bus bar, thereby closing the keying circuit. Accordingly, simple switch action is used in this design. A typical keyswitch assembly is illustrated in Fig. 2-9. Poor contact action can be caused by accumulation of lint, dust, or other foreign matter. In

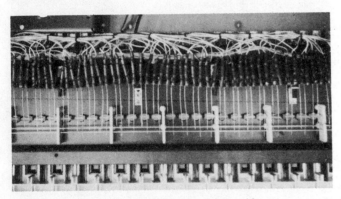

Fig. 2-9. Typical keyswitch assembly.

preventive maintenance procedures, the contact surfaces are kept in good condition by rubbing with a pipe cleaner moistened in benzine. TV-tuner contact cleaners may also be used.

An example of the variable-resistance keyswitch, used by Baldwin, is shown in Fig. 2-10. This is called a continuously variable graphite-track design. It normally provides a resistance change from 50k to

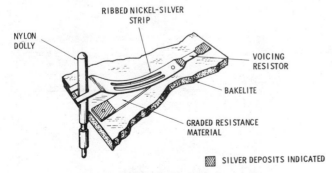

Fig. 2-10. Variable-resistance switch.

zero ohms as a key is depressed. Poor response can usually be corrected by cleaning the operating surfaces with benzine. Special fluids such as those used for cleaning volume and tone controls are suitable. The fluid may be dispensed readily in cramped spaces by using a control gun. Fig. 2-11 shows another type of variable-resistance keyswitch. This design is similar to that described above, except that

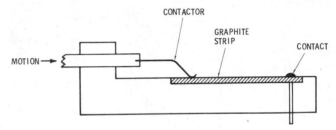

Fig. 2-11. Slide-action variable-resistance keyswitch.

slide action is used to obtain the resistance variation and switching sequence. Preventive maintenance consists of wiping the operating surface with a pipe cleaner moistened with benzine or an equivalent solvent. We will also find variable-resistance key switches that employ wire-wound resistors instead of graphite elements, as shown in Fig. 2-12. As be-

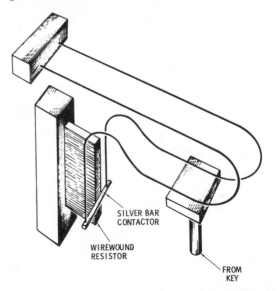

Fig. 2-12. Wirewound variable-resistance keyswitch design.

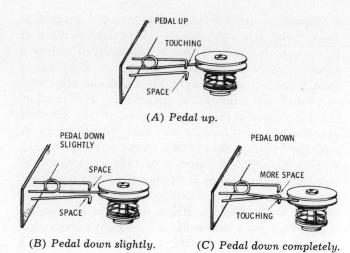

(A) *Pedal up.*

(B) *Pedal down slightly.* (C) *Pedal down completely.*

Fig. 2-13. Pedal switch action.

fore, preventive maintenance entails cleaning of the contact surfaces.

Pedal switches are basically the same as key switches. For example, Fig. 2-13 shows how a contact wire moves up and down to open and close the pedal circuit. In case of poor contact action, look for lint, dust, or other foreign matter on the contact surfaces. Volume is controlled by an expression bar or pedal, sometimes called a Swell shoe. Some organs use gradual-contact elements, such as the one shown in Fig. 2-11. If dirt particles accumulate on the contact surfaces, the sound output becomes noisy when

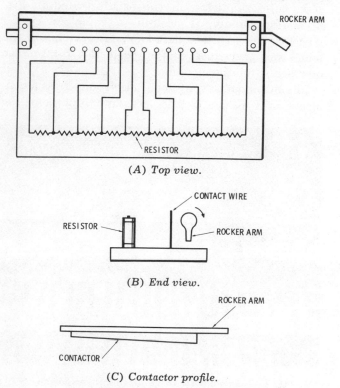

(A) *Top view.*

(B) *End view.*

(C) *Contactor profile.*

Fig. 2-14. Step-type resistance switch.

a steady tone is sounded and the expression pedal is depressed or released. Still another type of pedal switch is shown in Fig. 2-14. This design employs a number of fixed resistors that provide 1-dB steps of attenuation. As the rocker arm is turned, the contactor successively short-circuits the series of resistors. Cleaning procedure is basically the same as for keyswitches, which was explained earlier.

LESLIE SPEAKERS

One of the basic types of auxiliary tone cabinets is the Baldwin-Leslie design, illustrated in Fig. 2-15. Preventive maintenance entails lubrication of the upper tremulant rotor once each year. The oil hole at the center of the tremulant assembly is marked for

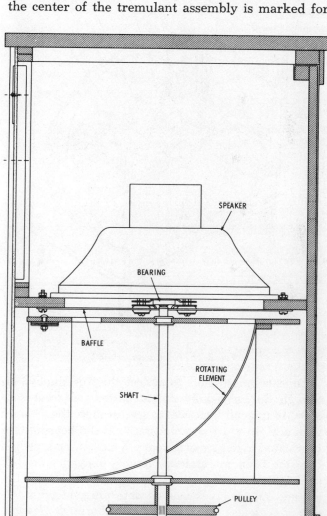

Fig. 2-15. Plan of Baldwin-Leslie auxiliary tone cabinet.

easy identification. Five drops of high-grade sewing-machine oil are recommended. Overflow should be carefully avoided; operating trouble will result if the pulley grooves or belts are contaminated by excess oil. In case the tone cabinet is in very frequent use, the rotor should be oiled at six-month intervals. The motor also requires lubrication; two oil tubes are provided for this purpose. About 25 drops of high-grade sewing-machine oil are placed in each tube at six-month intervals. However, under conditions of intensive operation, the motor should be lubricated at three-month intervals.

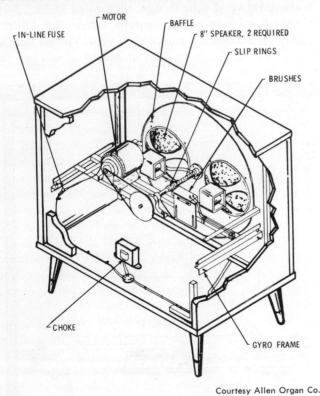

Courtesy Allen Organ Co.

Fig. 2-16. Allen gyro cabinet.

Tone cabinets tend to collect dust gradually; although this is usually not a matter for great concern, it is good practice to go through the cabinet with a blower at the same time that the bearings are lubricated. After several years, if a cleaning schedule has not been maintained, motors may accumulate sufficient lint and dust that ventilation becomes impaired and oil holes can become plugged with foreign substances. In such a case, a thorough cleaning is required to prevent rapid onset of serious trouble symptoms. Motors that have become clogged with lint and dust should be removed and cleaned with a solvent such as benzine, followed by lubrication. The interior of the cabinet should be cleared of dust, and the motor replaced, taking care that it is installed so that rotation is in the correct direction.

Preventive maintenance also includes inspection of the belts. If a belt shows signs of deterioration or fraying, or is slack, it should be replaced before a trouble symptom becomes obvious. In the case of gyro speakers, as shown in Fig. 2-16, the slip rings and brushes should also be inspected. These conduct the tone signals to the voice coils in the rotating speakers. The contacting surfaces should be clean, and the brushes should also press against the slip rings with sufficient force to provide good electrical contact. It is good practice to check mounting screws and nuts, to avoid the possibility of rattles at high volume levels. Finally, plugs should be checked to verify that they are fully inserted into the receptacles.

DISASSEMBLY NOTES

Many organs are designed so that the electronic components are accessible from the top of the instrument. The top portion of the console (fall board) is usually hinged so that it can be opened up and propped against the wall in back of the organ. In a typical situation, a large aluminum shield plate will then be exposed, as illustrated in Fig. 2-17. It is secured by several self-tapping screws; when the shield plate is removed, the circuit boards are accessible, as illustrated in Fig. 2-18. In this modern design, individual circuit boards are placed in slots, and slide out for quick removal, as illustrated in Fig. 2-19. Accordingly, if desired, a complete circuit board can be easily replaced. When servicing in the home, this procedure is often preferred to minimize down-time for the customer.

In older models, traditional electronic-chassis construction is used, and it is necessary to pinpoint the

Fig. 2-17. Shield plate covers electronic compartment behind manuals.

defective component before normal operation can be restored. Although this is a comparatively simple procedure in the case of a weak tube, some component defects and trouble situations challenge the best efforts of an experienced technician. Systematic troubleshooting procedures are explained subsequently. We will find that some components are readily accessible, whereas others may require rather

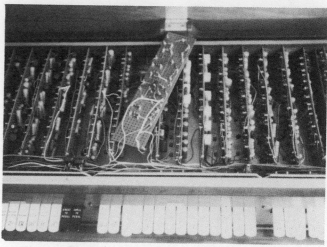

Fig. 2-19. Circuit boards slide out for quick removal.

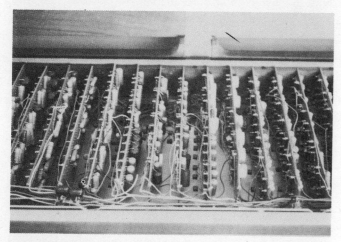

Fig. 2-18. Circuit boards are located under the top shield plate.

extensive disassembly procedures. For example, let us consider the procedure for replacement of the lower belt in the tone cabinet shown in Fig. 2-15. First, the large center-back and lower-compartment cover must be removed. Then, the bass speaker is dismounted and unplugged. (It must be lifted straight up for a short distance to avoid damaging the cone.) Next, the rotor support is removed from the drive shaft, and the new belt is placed on the large pulley. The belt is passed between the rotor and the shelf toward the driving motor.

With the new belt in preliminary position, next remove the motor-holding wing nut nearest the cabi-

net to partially drop the motor. The new belt can now be temporarily hooked over the screw that held the wing nut. This permits the bearing support to be replaced on the rotor shaft, and the ends of the support are positioned in the shallow locating channels provided at the speaker port. Next, align the holes in the support with the speaker mounting holes in the locating channels. In turn, the speaker can be placed back in position, and the two screws holding the speaker at each end of the bearing support can be replaced. These screws are not tightened at this time, and the remaining six screws are also replaced but not tightened. After all of the mounting screws have been started, they can be successively tightened. Then, place the new belt on the driving-motor pulley, and place the motor back in position. The wing nut is replaced, and the belt tension is adjusted as required. Although the belt must not slip, excessive tension must also be avoided to eliminate noisy operation and rapid wear. Excessive tension can also make rotor starting uncertain.

Chapter 3

Adjustments and Minor Repairs

Various adjustments are provided on all but the simplest electronic organs. These adjustments serve to balance sectional functions both from the standpoint of component tolerances and room acoustics. In some types of instruments, adjustments can be made in the voicing to imitate almost any design of pipe organ. If an organ is to be played in a church, or used for playing classical music, the vibratos are customarily "turned down" and the diapasons are emphasized. That is, a vibrato effect, in which the frequency of a musical tone is varied at a rate of six or seven times a second, is not in the pipe-organ tradition. Instead, the diapason tone color, which is fundamental in all organ music, has the classical pipe-organ timbre. Voicing adjustments are often made solely on the basis of personal preferences.

Tone cabinets usually have both low-frequency (woofer) and high-frequency (tweeter) speakers. An attenuator in the tweeter circuit permits the frequency balance of the sound output to be adjusted for individual preferences and to accommodate various room acoustics. The more elaborate types of tone cabinets may include a midrange speaker with a tweeter and a pair of bass speakers. In such a case, the midrange speaker circuit is also provided with an adjustable attenuator. Sometimes it is found that room acoustics are such that the frequency balance cannot be adjusted satisfactorily. This difficulty is most likely to be caused by standing-wave interference of certain bass tones. The cure is to relocate the tone cabinet(s) or the console.

Other adjustments are concerned with key and pedal actions. Both mechanical and electrical re-

quirements are involved. That is, a key might not be level with the other keys, although the switching action is normal. On the other hand, the switching action might be incorrect, although the key is level. In other cases, particularly when mounting or adjusting screws become loose, both mechanical and electrical problems arise. Sometimes a key or pedal becomes damaged by accidental striking with a heavy object. A repair job results, which could be minor or extensive, depending on the amount of damage that is involved.

VOICING ADJUSTMENTS

Voicing refers to the resultant tone output that is obtained through the mixing of various harmonics to imitate a musical instrument or other effect. This mixing process entails both frequency and amplitude considerations. That is, when a third harmonic is mixed with a fundamental, the harmonic frequency is three times that of the fundamental. Moreover, this third harmonic is necessarily added to the fundamental with a certain relative amplitude. The resultant tone output is characterized by both the frequency of the harmonic and by its amplitude. Amplitude adjustment is termed "setting a musical balance." So far as tone cabinets are concerned, setting a musical balance involves an adjustment of the relative treble and bass levels; an adjustment of the midrange level may also be included.

A typical tone-cabinet arrangement for the Rodgers organ is shown in Fig. 3-1. Two tone cabinets may be used, and located in opposite corners of a room, for example. These tone cabinets may also be supplemented by a Leslie acoustic-vibrato tone cabinet, as explained previously. Beginners should note that voicing adjustments and level settings are determined by the size, shape, and acoustic properties of the installation area. Although factory settings are made prior to shipment, these are merely average settings. Speaker adjustments alone will often help greatly in balancing an organ for a particular installation area. With reference to Fig. 3-1, the tweeter potentiometer is usually adjusted first. The recommended procedure is as follows.

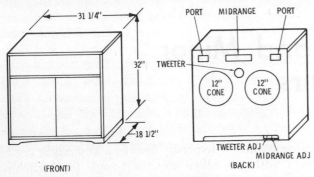

(A) *Front and back views showing location of adjustments.*

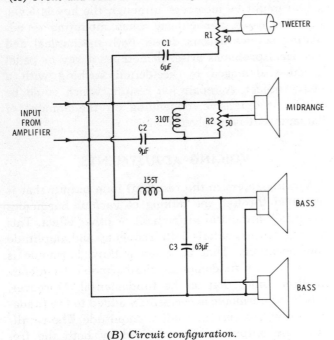

(B) *Circuit configuration.*

Fig. 3-1. Typical tone-cabinet arrangement.

Two persons are generally required—one to operate the instrument and one to adjust the speaker level controls. Potentiometer settings should be changed only while a continuous note or chord is being played. Obviously, the precise effect of changing a level adjustment with the instrument silent is unpredictable. This is the chief advantage of having two individuals available. A good chord to use in this procedure is the Middle C triad of C-E-G (Fig. 3-2). If the tone is too "bright," the setting of the tweeter potentiometer should be reduced; or, if the tone is too "dull," the setting should be increased. The mid-range potentiometer is then adjusted for optimum timbre. When there is considerable reverberation in the installation area, it is usually desirable to turn the tweeter potentiometer to a higher level than in a "dead" installation area. When two tone cabinets are used, it is helpful to disconnect one cabinet while the other is being adjusted. Finally, touch-up adjustments can be made, if required, with both cabinets operating.

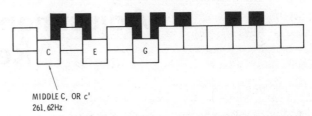

Fig. 3-2. Middle C triad of C-E-G.

Next, let us consider the console level adjustments for a typical organ, such as the one shown in Fig. 3-3. To make the pertinent level adjustments, the expression pedal is fully depressed, thereby providing maximum sound output. Then, the stop-rail piston is actuated to clear any existing presets, and to turn on the stop rail, preparatory to checking the tibia level. The organ mute must be turned off, because this piston softens nearly all the voices. Next, the following four Great stops are actuated: the 8' Tibia Clausa, the 4' Piccolo, the 2' Piccolo, and the Tibia ff. An assistant then plays any convenient chord on the Great manual, while the technician sets the tibia potentiometer on the output chassis to obtain a comfortably full-volume sound output. This tibia-level control, R31, is shown in Fig. 3-4.

The next step in balancing the voice levels in this example consists of setting the level of the main voices. First, cancel the Great stops that were actuated in the foregoing procedure, and actuate the following stops: the 8' Tibia Clausa (Great stop), the 8' Open Diapason (Solo stop), the Main ff, and the Tibia ff. An assistant plays any convenient chord on the Great manual, and then plays the same chord on the Solo manual, alternating back-and-forth to check the balance of the two sound outputs. The technician meanwhile adjusts the main-level control, R28, on the output chassis, shown in Fig. 3-4. This adjustment is made so that the apparent loudness of the Great sound output is approximately the same as that of the Solo sound output. The result is that the main voices are brought into balance with the tibia voices.

It has been noted previously that the tremulants may be turned down when an organ is installed in a church; since personal preferences vary, it is often desired to make tremulant adjustments in general installations. For the example under consideration, we may note that there are five stop tabs that affect the tremulants; these are termed the Main Tremulant (an amplitude modulation), the Main Vibrato (a frequency modulation), the Tibia Tremulant (an amplitude modulation), the Tibia Vibrato (a frequency modulation), and the Echo Vibrato, which is a built-in function of a Leslie speaker. If the locations of the tremulant-adjustment controls are not known, it is usually advisable to consult the organ service data. In the present example, the Tibia Tremulant is on the Tibia Rack, and the Main Tremulant is on the Tremulant Rack (see Fig. 3-5).

In the more elaborate organs, three adjustments may be provided for each tremulant, as seen in Fig. 3-6. These are the Speed (repetition rate) of the tremulant, the A-M Depth, and the FM Depth controls. Note that if an excessive depth of modu-

lation is used, the resulting overmodulation will cause interruptions in the tone with consequent thumping in the speaker. In simpler designs, the modulation depth is fixed, and only the vibrato rate can be adjusted (see Fig. 3-7, page 43). Of course, an experienced technician can easily change the depth of a tremulant by modifying resistor values in the modulator circuit. Modification is generally avoided, unless specifically requested and then it is general practice to recommend that an instrument be traded in on a more elaborate model.

In addition to the foregoing voicing adjustments, the more elaborately designed instruments may provide for adjustment of the formants (tone filters). For example, with reference to Fig. 3-8, the formants for the Tuba, Kinura, Vox Humana, and Bombarde reed voices are adjustable. Variable inductors L401, L402, L411, L412, L413, L431, L432, L433, L461, and L462 are the pertinent components. Thus, there are ten adjustments for the four voices noted in this example. The inductors are wound on ferrite cores, and have threaded caps. Adjustments are made by turning the caps. Since the coils are wound with very fine wire, care must be used not to press

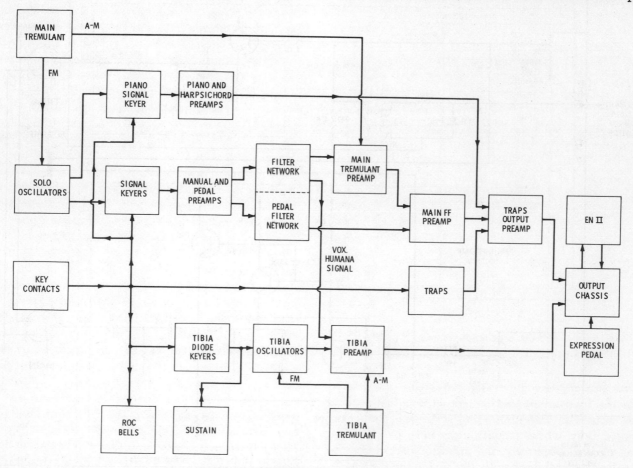

Fig. 3-3. Block diagram of a Rodgers organ.

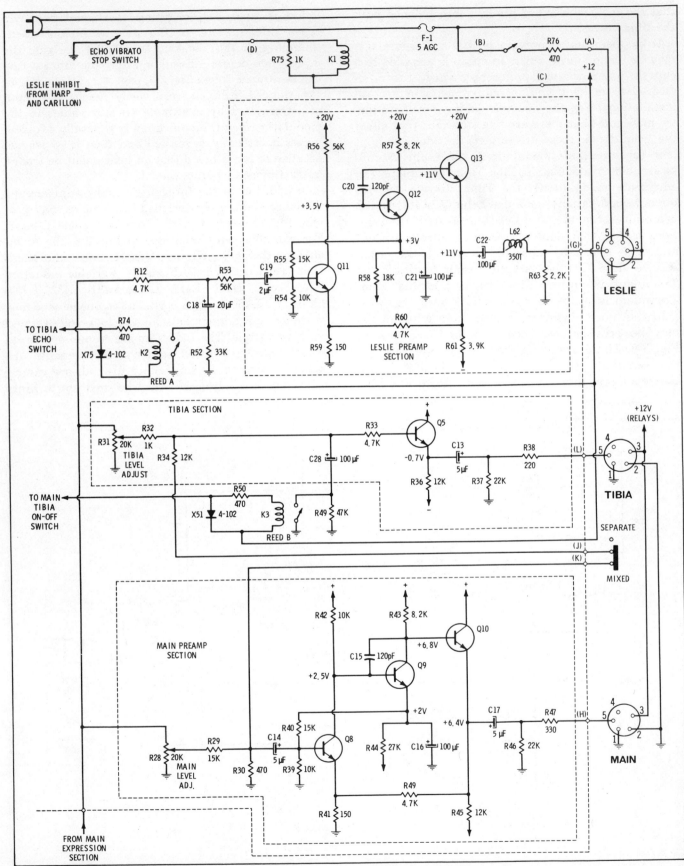

Fig. 3-4. Tibia-level and main-level output circuitry.

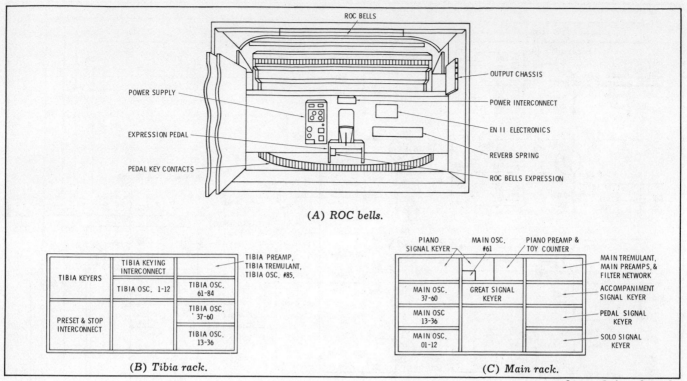

(A) *ROC bells.*

(B) *Tibia rack.*

(C) *Main rack.*

Courtesy Rodgers Organ Co.

Fig. 3-5. Typical sectional arrangement.

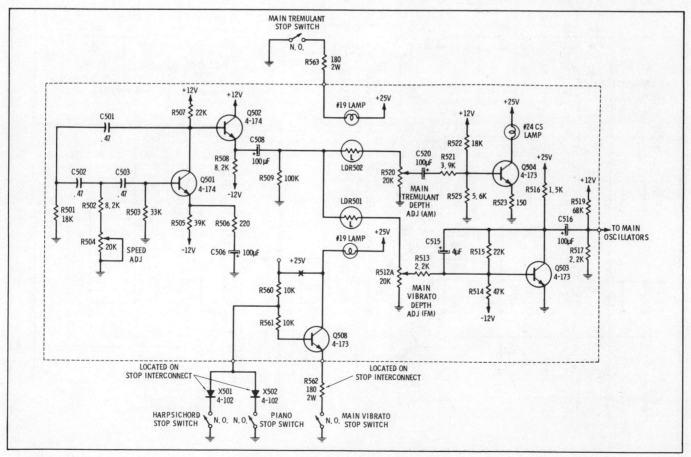

Fig. 3-6. A main-tremulant configuration.

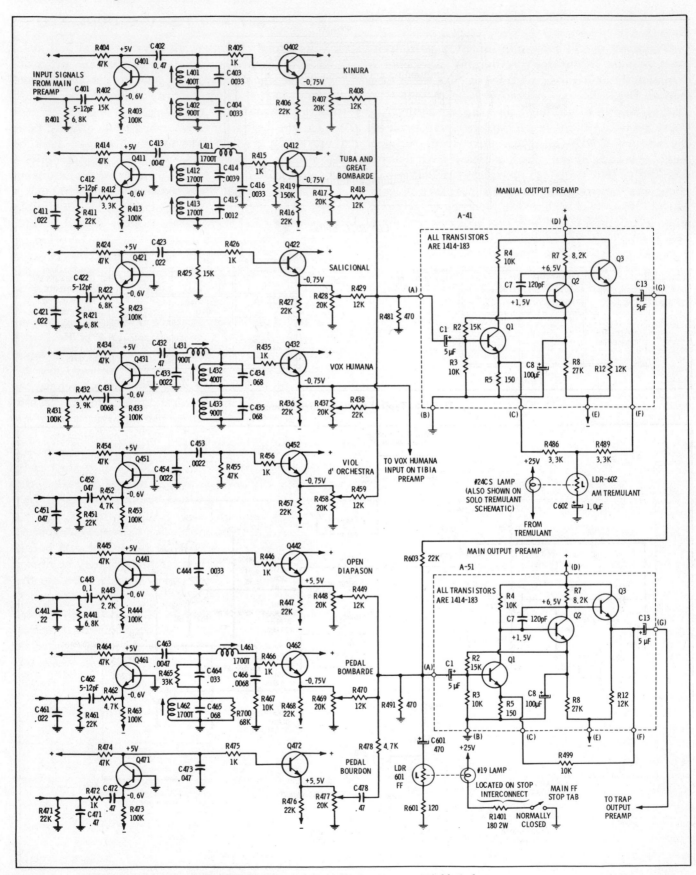

Fig. 3-8. Formant voicing adjustments are variable inductors.

against the leads while holding the cap between the fingers.

Beginners should avoid adjustment of voice formants, because it requires considerable experience to evaluate the musical significance of changes in filter action. Even the experienced technician will often find it advisable to "flag" the original settings by marking a line across each cap with white ink, or by affixing a strip of scotch tape. If the original angular setting of the "flag" is established, and the number of 180° turns are noted, the original adjustment can be precisely fixed for purposes of comparison. Note that in this example, each of the formants on a given voice interacts with the others in the group. Thus, in the Tuba adjustment, turning of formant cap L411 also affects the response of L412 and L413. As in all voicing adjustments, there are no absolute standards, because the color and quality of organ reeds are largely matters of individual taste.

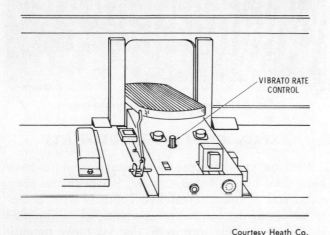

Courtesy Heath Co.

Fig. 3-7. Vibrato control located behind expression pedal.

It may appear to the apprentice that reed voices are rather "thin." The reason for this is that "body" is provided by the additive effect of the main voices. That is, the full ensemble will become "muddy" unless the reed voices are adjusted slightly on the "thin" side. Modern organ designers often provide a choice of speaker or headphone reproduction. If voicing adjustments are made with headphones, the test procedure will not annoy the customer or others in the vicinity. On the other hand, timbres are not quite the same in headphones as from a tone cabinet, and may be appreciably different. Therefore, after making voicing adjustments with headphones, the result should be checked using the tone cabinet(s). Note that a headphone balance control is commonly provided, to equalize the output and to compensate for possible differences in acuity between left and right ears.

KEY AND PEDAL ACTIONS

In normal operation, all keys are level and even, exert the same amount of spring pressure when depressed, dip equally, and start to produce a tone when approximately halfway down. A key should not rub against an adjoining key, and should not have any hesitancy in returning to its original position when released. The electrical contact must be continuously maintained while the key completes the latter portion of its downward travel, and during the initial portion of its upward travel. Although a key must not bind, neither should it be perceptibly loose. Most keyboard difficulties are caused by lint, dirt particles, or corrosion, and can be corrected by cleaning. However, problems can arise also because of loose screws, weak or broken springs, stripped threads, warped wooden rails, and deteriorated or disengaged felt pads.

Fig. 3-9 shows a typical key-leveling screw assembly. The screw is turned as required to bring the top surface of the key level with the other keys. Although the adjusting screw is secured only by friction in this arrangement, the threads seldom become loose. In the event that the adjusting screw might become loose, it can be secured in place by means of a coat of all-purpose cement over the threads. In this design, the leveling screw also serves to close the contacts of the dual-leaf contact strip when the key is depressed. In normal operation, the circuit is completed when the key travel is half completed, approximately. Deterioration of the felt pad is usually responsible for delayed engagement of the contacts. In such case, the pad should be replaced. Following pad replacement, it may be necessary to bend the spring leaves slightly to obtain the desired switch action.

In another arrangement, the dual-leaf contact strip is mounted behind the keys, as shown in Fig. 3-10. As noted previously, look for a deteriorated or disengaged felt pad in case the contacts close too

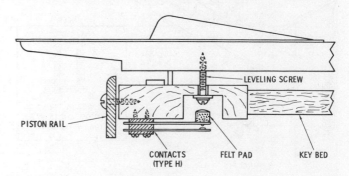

Courtesy Artisan Organs

Fig. 3-9. Key leveling-screw arrangement.

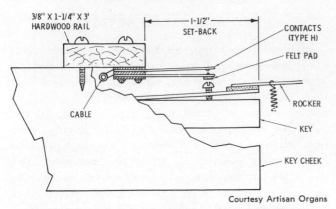

Fig. 3-10. Dual-leaf contact strip mounted behind keys.

Courtesy Artisan Organs

late. However, the same difficulty can be caused by warping of the hardwood rail, if the instrument has been exposed to conditions of excessively high humidity. A warped rail should be replaced, instead of attempting to compensate for the mechanical distortion by means of switch adjustments. With reference to Fig. 3-11, key travel is opposed by coil springs in most instruments. A spring may become weakened or broken if it becomes rusty; spring replacement is a simple matter, and the chief consideration is equality of tension compared with the other springs.

Fig. 3-12 illustrates the contact-wire and bus-bar type of switch contact. In this example, the bass keys actuate single contact wires, and the treble keys actuate double contact wires. In case of uncertain contact action, a strip of paper moistened in benzine can be inserted and then withdrawn after the key is depressed. (Emery cloth or other abrasives are not recommended for cleaning contacts.) The time of contact closure should also be checked.

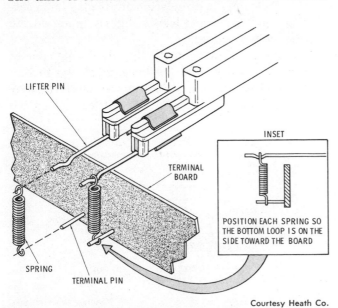

Courtesy Heath Co.

Fig. 3-11. Typical spring assembly.

As noted previously, key contacts normally close when the associated key is approximately halfway from top to bottom of its travel. In case the contacts are closed too late, or too early, a pair of thin-nose pliers should be used to grasp the contact wire near its mounting and to bend the wire up or down as required. Note that in case a contact wire is mounted on the key structure, it can become insecure due to a loose or defective pin-retaining clip (Fig. 3-13).

Fig. 3-12. Keyswitch contact arrangement.

EXPRESSION-PEDAL ADJUSTMENTS

Various types of expression-pedal assemblies have been used by various designers; however, the present trend is toward resistive controls with potentiometers as the control components, as exemplified in Fig. 3-14. This unit is a 10k log-taper potentiometer. The position of the expression-pedal bracket is adjusted so that the potentiometer lever will come to rest on the felt provided on the potentiometer-support bracket at both ends of the lever travel. Then, with the shoe fully depressed, the potentiometer shaft should be rotated so that zero ohms will be measured between terminal A and the center terminal. Next, as the shoe is released, the resistance normally increases. After the setscrews are tightened, a test is made by placing a 3/32" shim between the shoe and the felt down-stop. Now, the resistance normally measures 100 ohms (or somewhat more).

A common complaint after an organ has been in use for several years is that various pedals become squeaky. This can be caused by loose assembly screws, but more often by dry bearings. In the example of Fig. 3-14, the expression-pedal bushings should be lubricated with a light grease. It is also good foresight to apply a thin film of grease over all metallic surfaces that move against one another. Of

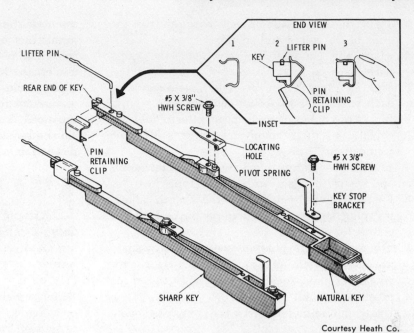

Fig. 3-13. Key assembly.

Courtesy Heath Co.

course, moving surfaces should slide freely, and shafts should turn easily in their bearings. If binding occurs, try loosening the pertinent assembly screws to determine whether there is a stressed mounting situation that can be relieved. Otherwise, a defective part that binds must be replaced.

CABLES AND CONNECTIONS

Tone cabinets are necessarily connected to their associated console by cables. These cables carry audio signals, and in the case of the more elaborate tone cabinets, also conduct control voltages and 117-volt ac power. In case of erratic operation, the cable connections (Fig. 3-15) should be checked. Sometimes a plug is not fully inserted into a receptacle, or recurrent mechanical stresses may cause the plug to fit loosely in its receptacle. In such a case, the plug and receptacle should be replaced. It is essential to make firm, soldered connections. After a cable

has been cut from a defective plug, proceed as follows to connect a new plug:

1. Remove the outer-cable sheath for an appropriate interval; for example, a plug typically requires 2½″ removal and a socket requires 1½″.
2. Remove insulation from leads: ⅞″ for a plug and ⅜″ for a socket, in this example.

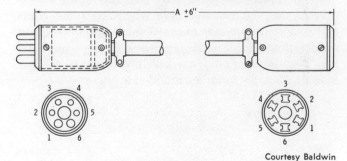

Courtesy Baldwin

Fig. 3-15. Tone-cabinet cable.

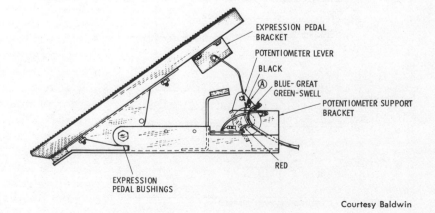

Fig. 3-14. Expression pedal assembly.

Courtesy Baldwin

3. Twist the loose ends of each wire, and tin the ends of the wires and shields.

4. Place the connector covers over the cable wires.

5. Slip ¾″ lengths of insulated sleeving over each wire prior to socket connections.

6. Insert the cable leads in proper terminals, according to their color code, and solder the connections.

7. Slip the insulation over the socket terminals and secure in place with plastic tape.

8. Fasten clamps securely on the sheath, allowing plug and socket to extend beyond end of connector cover ¼″.

9. Twist the cable plug or socket clockwise to normal position, press connector cover over connector, and lock in place with the three machine screws.

10. Using an ohmmeter, check the completed cable for continuity.

11. Clean the cable sheath and plug pins with alcohol.

12. Install cable, and route it so that it is not likely to be subject to accidental snagging or other mechanical forces.

Fig. 3-16 shows an example of cable color-coding. It also exemplifies how a pair of cable assemblies may be interconnected. Since the same color may be used for more than one wire, it is obviously necessary to use considerable care when replacing plugs and sockets in arrangements of this type. Continuity checks provide a conclusive check of the completed job. Beginners should not fall into the trap of confusing pin-side and terminal-side connection sequences. That is, with reference to Fig. 3-16, the numbers show the terminal sides of the sockets and show the pin sides of the plugs—this legend is included in the organ service data. Other drawings, such as the one in Fig. 3-15, show the number sequence for the terminal side of the plug, and for the terminal side of the socket. Therefore, the technician must strictly mind his p's and q's, if the completed job is to function normally.

LAMP CIRCUIT

Electronic organs, particularly in more elaborate designs, often have built-in lighting facilities to illuminate the pedal clavier and music rack. The former are generally tungsten lamps, and the latter may be fluorescent tubes. Both types require occasional replacement. At least one manufacturer also provides a built-in fluorescent lamp that can be turned on to identify the keys by means of letters and colors. This is a training aid for student performers. A pilot light is provided in most instruments to indicate when the main power switch is turned on. This may employ a neon bulb. As explained in greater detail subsequently, we will occasionally find tungsten lamps used as control devices in combination with light-dependent resistors (LDRs).

Fig. 3-17 shows a lighting configuration in which all the bulbs except one are connected into an adjustable dimmer circuit that employs taps on the secondary winding of the power transformer. However, the pedal light is connected directly across the 117-volt line in this example. In other designs, a separate on-off switch may be provided for the pedal

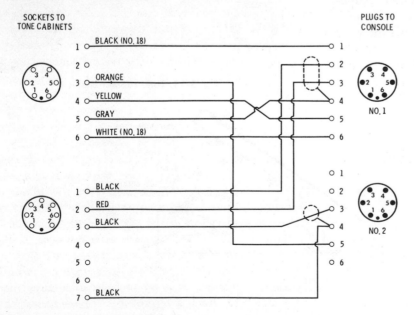

Fig. 3-16. Example of cable color code.

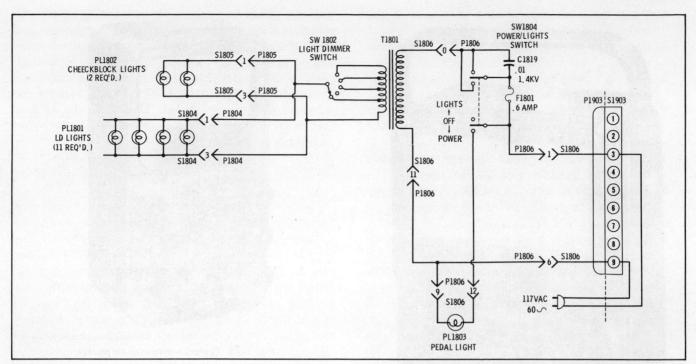

Courtesy Thomas Organ Co.

Fig. 3-17. Lighting circuitry.

light. Fluorescent lamps are preferred for illuminating music racks; a typical configuration is shown in Fig. 3-18. When a lamp is nearing the end of its useful life, the inner surface of the glass becomes discolored, and the light output is diminished. Eventually, the lamp will flicker intermittently, or become completely inoperable.

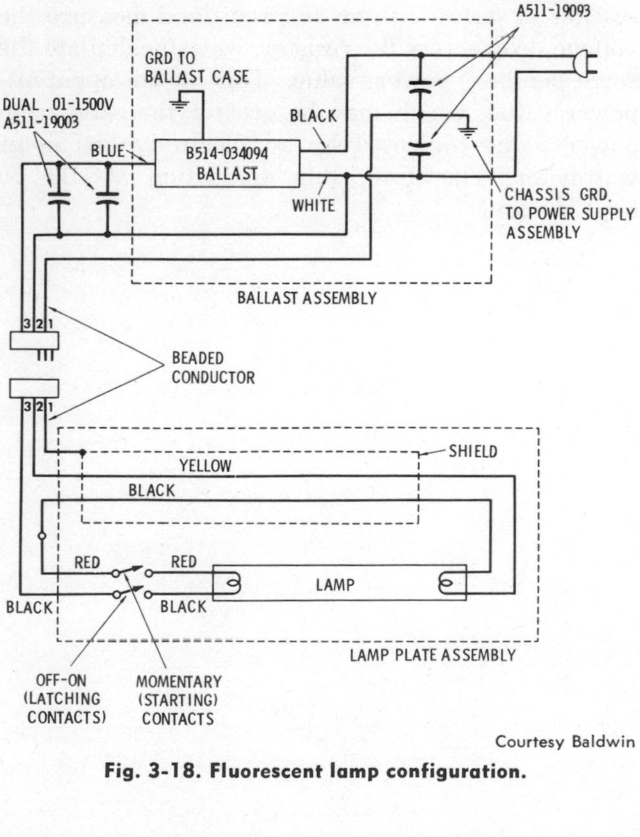

FUSES

Power-supply circuits are always fused. For example, see F1801 in Fig. 3-17. In many cases, slow-blow fuses are used. Fuse locations can be determined by referring to the organ service data. In nearly all cases, a fuse does not blow unless there is a circuit defect present that imposes an abnormal current demand. Therefore, it is usually necessary to troubleshoot the circuitry before a new fuse will "hold." As explained in greater detail subsequently, the quickest way to localize the trouble is to disconnect the output leads from the power supply. If the new fuse blows, the trouble is in the power supply. Or, if the power supply is operating normally, we reconnect the loads one-by-one until the abnormal demand is imposed that causes the new fuse to blow. Then, the trouble will be found in the abnormal-demand branch. Always replace a fuse with the type and value specified in the service data. Never short-circuit a fuse holder, as extensive damage is likely to result. By the same token, never use a screwdriver to "spark" a circuit to determine whether power is present. A good technician always uses a voltmeter to check a circuit.

Courtesy Baldwin

Fig. 3-18. Fluorescent lamp configuration.

Fig. 3-19. A VOM is generally used to check organ circuitry.

Fig. 3-20. Typical wattmeter-voltmeter.

A VOM such as that illustrated in Fig. 3-19 is convenient for checking organ circuitry, since it does not use a power cord, and both test leads can be operated above ground potential. Similarly, battery-operated FET meters provide operating convenience. The chief limitation of this class of instruments is lack of alternating current indication. Although indirect methods can be used to measure alternating current with a VOM, experienced technicians generally prefer a wattmeter, such as the one illustrated in Fig. 3-20. It may be noted that this type of wattmeter is an electrodynamometer instrument, which indicates true-power values. If we connect a power resistor in series with an ac circuit and measure the voltage drop across the resistor, we can calculate the corresponding power value. This is an apparent-power value, which may be greater than the true-power value indicated by an electrodynamometer wattmeter. Therefore, this distinction should be kept in mind.

Chapter 4

Tone-Generator Troubleshooting

A tone generator is a device that generates the electrical waveforms that are usually modified, then amplified, and finally converted into sound waves by one or more loudspeakers. The term *solo* denotes a single voice or instrument that plays a melody; an equivalent term is *swell*. The simplest type of tone generator is a solo oscillator; it produces a given note as a solo tone. A more elaborate form of tone generator produces two notes simultaneously; the two pitches are separated by an octave. Still another type of tone generator produces two electrical waveforms that have the same pitch, but different waveshapes. For example, the tone generator might provide a sine-wave output and a pulse output.

Some tone generators can oscillate at more than one frequency, depending on which of three adjacent keys is depressed. There are tone generators that are keyed on or off by changes in bias or supply voltage, whereas other tone generators operate continuously, with the keying circuits in the audio output leads. In either case, the tone generators may be classed as electronic or electromechanical types; since most organs in current use have electronic tone-generating devices, this basic design is stressed in the following discussion. We often classify tone generators into Swell, Great, and Pedal groups, as exemplified in Fig. 4-1. Note, however, that the classification is not exclusive, inasmuch as the coupler circuits permit a Swell generator or a Great generator (or both) to operate in combination with a Pedal generator.

TONE-GENERATOR ARRANGEMENTS AND IDENTIFICATION

When one or more notes are "dead," the trouble may be traced to an inoperative tone generator. However, the fault could also be due to dirty or corroded switch contacts, or to a defect in a power-supply branch. Therefore, systematic troubleshooting procedures are usually required to close in on the defective component. The three basic tools in trouble analysis are the schematic diagram, an oscilloscope, and a VOM. Note that schematic diagrams for all but the simplest types of organs are very complex, and cannot be printed on a sheet of reasonable size. Accordingly, the schematics are sectionalized and printed on twenty or thirty 8½ × 11" or 11 × 17" sheets. In addition, the organ service manual may include thirty to forty pages of general information, speaker interconnections, adjustments, technical descriptions, and service bulletins. Before any troubleshooting is attempted on a specific model, the service data should be carefully reviewed.

READING SCHEMATIC DIAGRAMS

Although the schematic diagram for a tone generator is printed on one page in the service data, it should not be assumed that all of the generator components will be found on a single subchassis or PC board in the organ. For example, Fig. 4-2 shows how the tuned tank circuit for a tone generator may be packaged in an individual housing, which is mounted with a number of similar housings in a subchassis. From the subchassis, a cable is routed to a PC board at the other end of the organ, which mounts the transistors and remaining components of the tone generators. An elaborate organ may have a complement of 158 oscillators (tone generators), with subgrouping into 85 tibia oscillators and 73 main oscillators. Fig. 4-3 is the circuit for a main oscillator; each main oscillator has the same circuitry, although com-

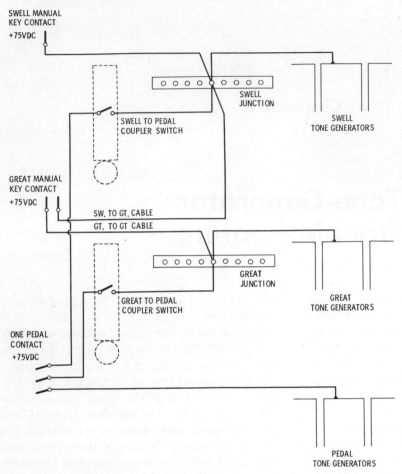

Courtesy Artisan Organs

Fig. 4-1. Basic flow chart.

ponent values vary from one unit to another.

In the foregoing example, the main oscillators (also called solo oscillators) operate in a system with the block diagram shown in Fig. 4-4. Layout diagrams may or may not be provided to supplement the schematic diagrams. A layout diagram serves to show the physical locations of the tone-generator groups and subgroups, as seen in Fig. 4-5. If a layout diagram is not available for an unfamiliar organ, the technician must study the schematic diagrams, and observe the cabling routes to identify the func-

Fig. 4-2. Tuned tank for a tone generator may be packaged separately.

tional sections. Individual oscillators may be identified by guide numbers stenciled on the generator rack frames. For example, the bottom panel of the right-hand section of the tibia rack shown in Fig. 4-5 contains the numbered oscillators shown in Fig. 4-6.

In the foregoing example, tone-generator identification is facilitated by provision of a keying chart (Fig. 4-7). This diagram shows the oscillators keyed by any given manual or pedal key with any given stop. Thus, Middle C (Key 25) will key oscillator 25 with an 8′ stop depressed. Or, it will key oscillator 37 with a 4′ stop down; with a 16′ stop depressed, it will key oscillator 13. Let us suppose that in a trouble situation, Key 25 functions normally except when a 4′ stop is depressed. This symptom points to a defect in oscillator 37. Accordingly, we turn our attention to the main oscillator section 37–60 shown in Fig. 4-5. Then, oscillator 37 can be pinpointed by means of the guide numbers printed on this rack frame. Although the technician will not always find complete supplementary data for the schematic diagrams in an organ service manual, he will be able

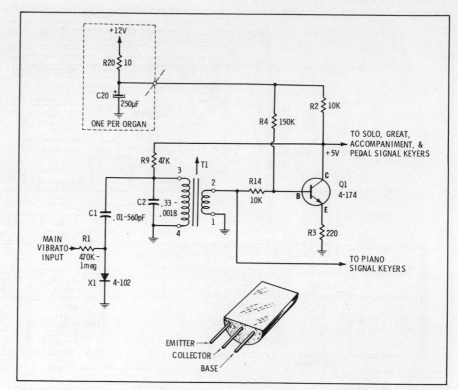

Fig. 4-3. Typical configuration for a main oscillator.

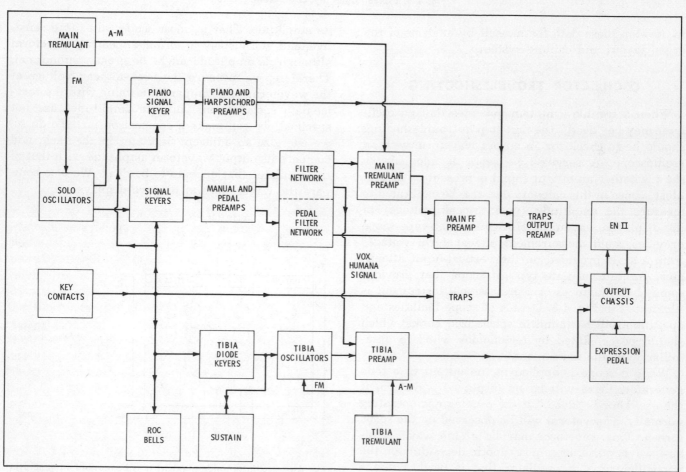

Fig. 4-4. Complete block diagram of an organ.

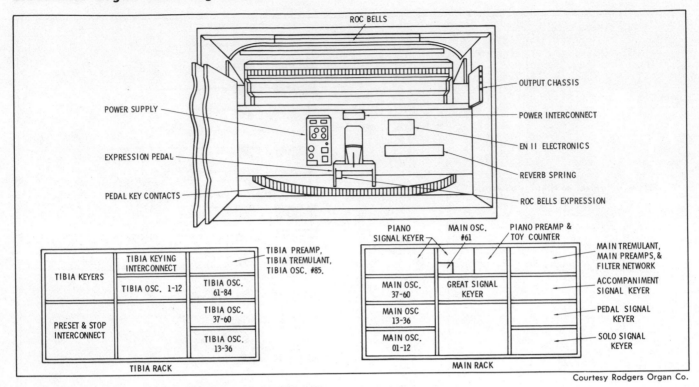

Courtesy Rodgers Organ Co.

Fig. 4-5. Typical organ layout diagram.

to develop these data for himself by analysis of the organ layout and cabling system.

OSCILLATOR TROUBLESHOOTING

When a trouble symptom indicates that an oscillator may be "dead," the first step in troubleshooting should be to check for an output waveform with an oscilloscope. A service-type scope is adequate to show whether an output signal is present or absent. Most scopes in this category can also be calibrated to measure the amplitude (peak-to-peak voltage) of the displayed waveform. However, a lab-type scope provides rapid measurement of waveform voltages from a scale provided on the vertical-input attenuator. An intermediate type of scope that provides some of the features of a professional instrument is illustrated in Fig. 4-8. Details of scope facilities and operation will be found in specialized books, which should be consulted by technicians who are unfamiliar with the instrument.

When a scope is applied at the output of a tone generator, there will be no displayed waveform if the oscillator is "dead." If the oscillator is operating normally, a waveform will be observed on the scope screen. This waveform may be a sine wave, semi-sine wave, pulse, or semisawtooth, depending on the particular type of oscillator that is used. When a waveform is displayed, we are also concerned with

its amplitude. That is, most scopes are quite sensitive, and will display a normal-appearing waveform although its amplitude might be greatly subnormal. Therefore, we measure the peak-to-peak voltage of the waveform, and compare this value with the service-data specifications. In case amplitudes are not specified, we can make a comparison test. To do so, we energize an adjacent oscillator in the rack, and compare its output waveform amplitude with that of the oscillator that appears to be dead. We also compare the waveshapes of the two displays.

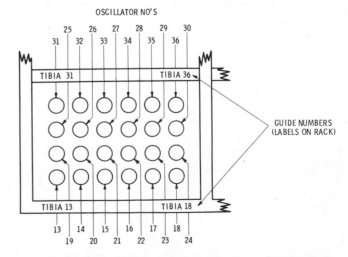

Fig. 4-6. Oscillator guide numbers may be marked on generator rack frames.

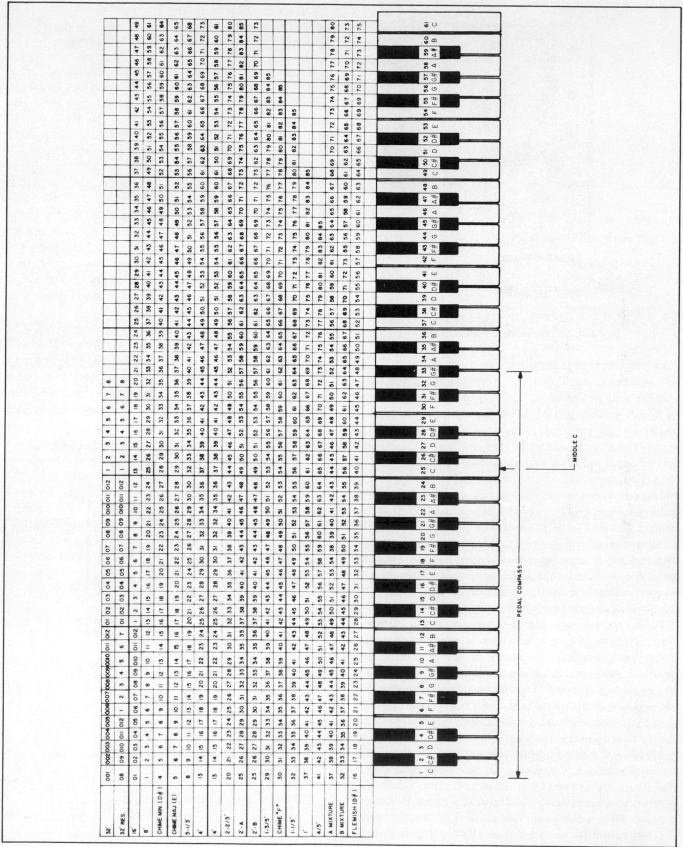

Fig. 4-7. Keying chart.

Courtesy Rodgers Organ Co.

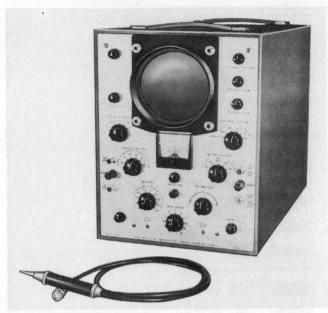

Courtesy Simpson Electric Co.

Fig. 4-8. An intermediate type of scope.

In the event that the output waveform from the suspected oscillator has normal amplitude, the trouble will be found in the output circuit from the oscillator to the utilization device, or possibly in the utilization device itself. This area of troubleshooting is covered subsequently. In this chapter, we are concerned with analysis and repair of defective oscillators. The approach is somewhat different for solid-state, vacuum-tube, and gas-tube oscillators, and is quite different for electromechanical generators. Since practically all present-day production entails solid-state designs, it is appropriate to start our troubleshooting discussion with transistor tone generators. We will find that solid-state designs generally employ numerous semiconductor diodes, many of which operate as electronic switches.

With reference to Fig. 4-9, notice that a Hartley configuration is employed, with a core-tuned tank. Since the operating frequency of the oscillator depends to some extent upon the load demand, a buffer stage is provided between the oscillator transistor and the output load bus. Note that a buffer stage is not provided between the oscillator transistor and the first frequency divider. The reason is that the frequency divider imposes a fixed load on the oscillator, whereas the output load bus is keyed, which results in sudden changes of load demand. Diode X1 is reverse-biased when the vibrato input is not in use. Therefore, the diode "looks like" an open switch. On the other hand, when the vibrato input is employed, the diode becomes forward-biased, and conducts the vibrato waveform into the oscillator tank

circuit. This variation modulates the oscillator output tone signal. Note that all of the master oscillators utilize the same circuit, with different L and C values.

When an oscillator is "dead" as indicated by a scope test, the first question is whether collector supply voltage is present. Accordingly, we measure the supply voltage (+15 volts in the example of Fig. 4-9) with a VOM or equivalent type of dc voltmeter. This test serves to distinguish between oscillator trouble and power-supply trouble. In case normal power-supply voltage is present, the oscillator circuit components should be examined. Statistically, fixed capacitors are the most probable troublemakers. If a capacitor such as C3 is suspected of being open, it can be quick-checked by bridging with a known good capacitor to see if oscillator operation is resumed. If the oscillator starts up, replace C3, and the job is completed except for possible checking of the oscillating frequency.

Next, let us consider the situation in which C3 in Fig. 4-9 is shorted. In this case, transistor Q1A will be burned out, due to application of +15 volts to its base, which causes a greatly excessive current through the base-emitter junction to ground. Accordingly, both C3 and Q1A must be replaced in this

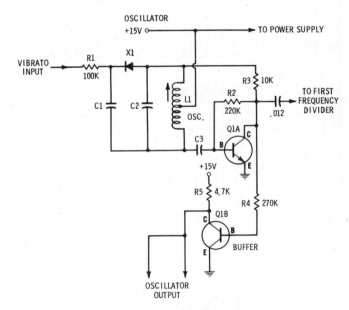

MASTER OSCILLATOR TUNING COMPONENTS				
GENS.	C1	C2	C3	L1
C#-D	.039	.022	.0068	P-9978-3
D#-E	.033	.018	.0056	P-9978-3
F-F#	.027	.015	.0047	P-9978-3
G-G#	.022	.012	.0039	P-9978-2
A-A#	.018	.01	.0033	P-9978-2
B-C	.015	.0082	.0027	P-9978-2

Fig. 4-9. Transistor tone-generator configuration.

situation. In the event that the trouble is being caused by leakage or a short-circuit in C2, one end of the capacitor must be disconnected for test, because it is shunted by the comparatively low winding resistance of L1. If the 0.012-μF coupling capacitor becomes leaky, the oscillator frequency tends to drift because of a shift in the collector voltage of Q1A. Of course, if the coupling capacitor opens up, the first frequency divider becomes inoperative. This removal of oscillator circuit capacitance also causes the oscillator frequency to increase. Frequency measurement and tuning adjustments are explained subsequently.

Although the normal dc voltages are not shown for component terminals in Fig. 4-9, it is easy to determine these values by comparison with an adjacent oscillator that is operating normally. In this example, the oscillator operates continuously, whereas an oscillator in another type of organ may be keyed off and on. However, this is a matter of operational detail, not of functional distinction. When an oscillator is keyed off and on, the schematic diagram often indicates the on and off collector-voltage values. For example, a typical keyed-oscillator transistor normally has a collector voltage of +6.5 volts while it is keyed on, and zero volts while it is keyed off.

Note in passing that an oscillator transistor may sometimes *seem* to be reverse-biased on the basis of dc-voltmeter measurements. This is found both in blocking oscillators and in Hartley oscillators operated in Class C. Fig. 4-10 shows the circuit action that is involved. In this example, an npn transistor is connected in a simple transformer feedback configuration. Tight coupling is employed between the collector and base coils, so that there is a large amount of feedback voltage. The collector and base waveforms show the sequence of circuit action. At the instant that the transistor comes out of collector-current cutoff, the circuit oscillates for one-half cycle. Because of the heavy feedback (overdrive), a large amount of base current is drawn during the half cycle of oscillation. This current charges C1 as shown in Fig. 4-10C. The transistor is cut off, but eventually comes out of cutoff as C1 discharges through R1, and the operating cycle is repeated.

It follows from Fig. 4-10C that a dc voltmeter will indicate the average value of base voltage indicated by the dotted line. Since this is a negative voltage, we would conclude that the npn transistor is reverse-biased—and on the average, this is true. However, it is evident that the transistor is not cut off continuously; that is, during the half cycles of conduction, the transistor conducts briefly and heavily. Of

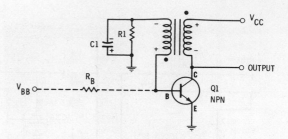

(A) Circuit diagram.

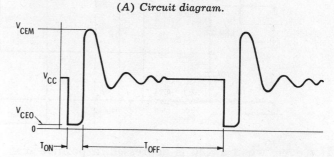

(B) Collector-voltage waveform.

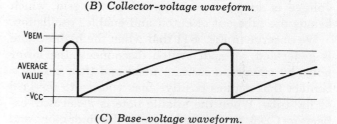

(C) Base-voltage waveform.

Fig. 4-10. Transistor blocking oscillator.

course, if the oscillator is "dead" for any reason, the base voltage measures practically zero, because this is a signal-developed bias. Note that the operating frequency of a blocking oscillator does not depend on the inductance values of the transformer windings. Instead, the oscillating frequency is determined by the time constant R1C1. Therefore, a tone generator that employs a blocking oscillator customarily provides a variable resistance for R1. Alternatively, an auxiliary fixed-bias source can be used and applied via R_B. If R_B is made variable, the oscillating frequency can be adjusted thereby.

Many vacuum-tube tone generators are still in use. Consequently, the features of concern to the organ technician are covered in this section. Fig. 4-11 shows a typical configuration. A basic Hartley feedback circuit is used, which can oscillate at any one of three frequencies corresponding to three consecutive notes. If two keys are depressed simultaneously, only the higher of the two pitches will be reproduced; or if three keys are depressed simultaneously, only the highest pitch will be sounded. The oscillating frequency depends upon the amount of effective capacitance that is switched across the inductor. Note that the tube is normally cathode-biased beyond cutoff so that the circuit does not oscillate.

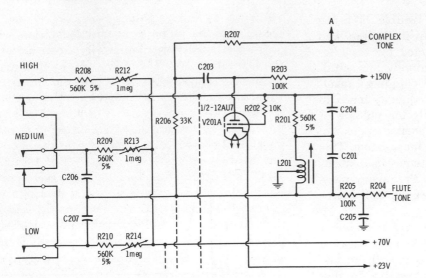

Fig. 4-11. Vacuum-tube oscillator configuration.

However, when a key is depressed, a positive bias voltage is automatically applied to the grid, which brings the tube out of cutoff and enables oscillation.

We observe in Fig. 4-11 that when the highest note is generated, an spdt switch disconnects the lower notes by opening a series contact and then closing a contact that applies positive bias voltage to the grid of the tube. When the middle note is generated, capacitor C206 is shunted across the inductor, and enabling bias is also applied to the tube. When the lowest note is generated, capacitor C207 is shunted across the inductor, and enabling bias is also applied to the tube. Coarse tuning is provided by core adjustment in L201. Fine tuning is provided by potentiometers R212, R213, and R214, which determine the exact value of enabling bias voltage for the individual keys. The output from the inductor is almost a sine wave, and provides a flute tone. On the other hand, the capacitively coupled output from the plate is a complex waveform with greatly accentuated harmonics.

As in the case of a transistor tone generator, a scope is the most convenient instrument for checking a suspected "dead" oscillator. In case no output waveform is present, the supply voltages should be checked next with a VOM or equivalent instrument. The tube is the prime suspect, and is usually checked by substitution. Next to defective tubes, leaky capacitors are the most common troublemakers. In this example, a leaky capacitor will cause incorrect circuit voltages, with the exception of C201. A capacitor that is shunted by a coil must have one end disconnected for test. Voltages at any point in the circuit can be checked by comparison with an adjacent oscillator that is in normal working condition.

Note that oscillator coils are generally wound with very fine wire. Therefore, if a shorted tube or ca-

pacitor causes excessive current demand through the coil, it is likely to burn out. This defect will cause incorrect circuit voltages, and can be definitely confirmed by a continuity test with an ohmmeter. Avoid the use of continuity testers that supply substantial test currents. When a coil is replaced, it may be necessary to adjust the core gap. That is, if a potentiometer tuning control will not bring a note into tune, the core gap should be changed to permit correct pitch adjustment at about the mid-range setting of the potentiometer. Of course, capacitor defects can simulate an incorrectly adjusted core gap. Tuning procedures are explained in greater detail subsequently.

Neon bulbs are used in some tone generators; since neon bulbs are also used as frequency dividers and as electronic switches, the beginner must be careful to avoid confusion among these functions. A basic neon-bulb tone generator is shown in Fig. 4-12. The initial approach to trouble analysis is much the same as for transistor or tube-type oscillators. That is, it is advisable to use a scope to check for presence or absence of (or greatly attenuated) output. The supply voltage should be checked with a dc voltmeter. The most likely cause of oscillator failure or abnormal operation is leaky capacitors. However, a neon bulb, like a vacuum tube, has a definite useful life span, and should be checked by substitution in case the other circuit components are not defective. Note that an exact replacement is desirable, because an organ manufacturer selects the neon bulbs used in production and also puts them through a stabilizing and aging process.

Electromechanical tone generators such as the one shown in Fig. 4-13 will be encountered occasionally. If a scope check at a coil output terminal shows that there is no tone waveform present, the trouble may

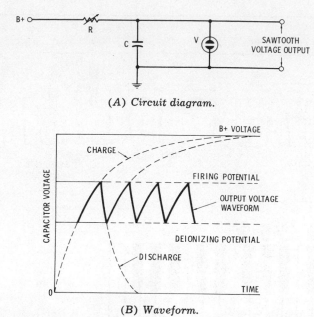

(A) *Circuit diagram.*

(B) *Waveform.*

Fig. 4-12. Neon-bulb sawtooth-waveform generator.

be either mechanical or electrical. It is not easy to observe whether a tone wheel is rotating or not, but a definite test can be made by touching the wheel with a fingertip. Most of the tone generators have more than one wheel mounted on the same shaft. Therefore, if a shaft is not turning, more than one note will be "dead." Synchronous-motor drive is used, and a motor repair or replacement is generally involved. Weak output, with normal tone-wheel rotation, may be due to a loose magnet that has drifted back from the circumference of the wheel. In such a case, a simple adjustment serves to restore normal output. On the other hand, a damaged or burned-out coil is difficult to replace, because of the involved procedure in disassembly and reassembly of the generator. It is recommended in this situation that the entire generator be returned to the factory.

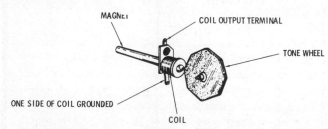

Fig. 4-13. Electromechanical tone-generator arrangement.

OSCILLATOR TUNING ADJUSTMENTS

Tuning can be done by ear, or with the aid of various tuning devices. A professional technician, preferably one with a musical background, can tune an organ by ear as satisfactorily as by any other means. On the other hand, the technician with an untrained musical ear must rely upon suitable instrumentation. An elementary error often made by technician apprentices is to retune an oscillator when the trouble is actually caused by a defective component in the output load system. For example, if a diode in the oscillator load circuit develops a poor front-to-back ratio, the pitch of the sound output is likely to shift. (See X1 in Fig. 4-3.) At the same time, some other functional trouble is present, but might be overlooked unless a thorough check-out has been made. Thus, it might be found that there is little or no vibrato response associated with the off-pitch note. An experienced technician will correct the functional difficulty before assuming that tone-generator retuning is required.

From a technical standpoint, organ tuning is easier than piano tuning, because organ notes are sustained. The flute voice is preferred, because it approximates a pure sine waveform and is easier to evaluate for pitch. A standard starting point is the C tone generator, which should be tuned precisely to 523.3 Hz. Among frequency standards, the tuning fork is basic. It is simply a U-shaped metal device with a handle at the bottom. When struck, a tuning fork radiates a pure note of constant pitch; it may be mounted on a hollow box to obtain acoustic amplification. The next step in elaboration is provision of electromagnetic drive, so that the fork is maintained in constant vibration. An amplifier may also be added to provide high-level sound output.

Depending on the design of the organ, it may be necessary to tune only one octave; that is, some organs use only one octave of tone generators, supplemented by frequency dividers. As explained previously, another design might employ 158 tone generators. It is helpful to start with consideration of a simple design in which only one octave requires tuning. The procedure is conveniently divided into two parts called "rough tuning" and "fine tuning." We start tone-generator adjustments with the rough-tuning sequence. Extensive use is made of the "beat note" that is produced when two notes of almost the same frequency are applied to the speaker. A beat note increases and decreases in its intensity at a rate that is determined by the frequency difference between the two notes. For example, if a 440-Hz tone is mixed with a 442-Hz tone, a throbbing sound, which varies at the rate of 2 Hz, will be heard. Again, if a 440-Hz tone is mixed with a 438-Hz tone, a 2-Hz beat is heard. "Zero beat," or no intensity change occurs when both notes have the same frequency, such as when both are 440-Hz tones.

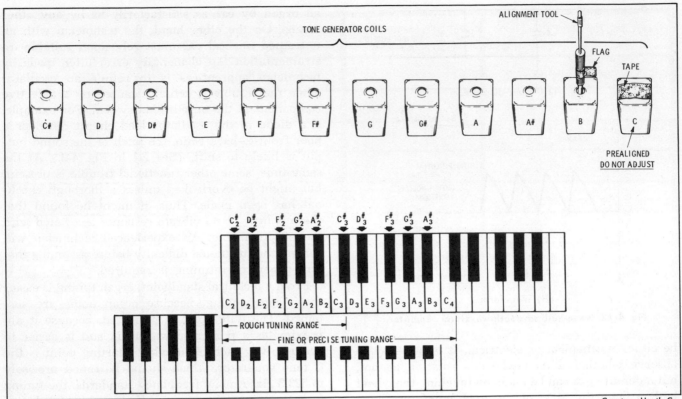

Fig. 4-14. Reference data for tuning procedure.

Courtesy Heath Co.

In this example, tuning is accomplished by adjusting slugs in oscillator coils. An alignment tool is used to turn the slugs. With reference to Fig. 4-14, the rough-tuning process is as follows:

1. Depress the flute tab switch, and turn all other tab switches off.
2. The lower octave notes of the Swell keyboard are used; beginners may find it helpful to mark the keys as shown in Fig. 4-14. A small piece of masking tape will take pencil or ink, and can be secured to the key without leaving a stain.
3. The C note is zero beat with a tuning fork or equivalent standard; or, in some cases, it is accepted as a reference without checking its absolute pitch.
4. It is helpful to tape a small flag on the alignment tool, as pictured in Fig. 4-14. The flag indicates how far each slug has been turned.
5. Play the B2 note (immediately to the left of C3). Compare its pitch with that of the C generator by playing C3. Adjust the slug in oscillator B for zero beat.
6. Play notes B2 and C3 simultaneously, and if no throbbing is audible, note the position of the flag, and turn the alignment tool clockwise by the number of turns stipulated in the rough-

ZERO BEAT		THEN ADJUST GENERATOR COIL CLOCKWISE	
1.	(✓) B2 with C3	B	1-3/4 turns
2.	(✓) A#2 with B2	A#	2-1/4 turns
3.	( ) A2 with A#2	A	1-3/4 turns
4.	( ) G#2 with A2	G#	2 turns
5.	( ) G2 with G#2	G	2-1/4 turns
6.	( ) F#2 with G2	F#	1-3/4 turns
7.	( ) F2 with F#2	F	2 turns
8.	( ) E2 with F2	E	2-1/4 turns
9.	( ) D#2 with E2	D#	1-3/4 turns
10.	( ) D2 with D#2	D	2 turns
11.	( ) C#2 with D2	C#	2-1/4 turns

Courtesy Heath Co.

Chart 4-1. Rough Tuning Chart

PLAY NOTES	TURN CLOCKWISE	BEATS IN 10 SECONDS	BEATS IN 30 SECONDS
1. ( ) C3 and G3	G	9	26
2. ( ) G2 and D3	D	7	20
3. ( ) D3 and A3	A	10	29
4. ( ) A2 and E3	E	7	23
5. ( ) E3 and B3	B	11	33
6. ( ) B2 and F#3	F#	8	25
7. ( ) F#2 and C#3	C#	6	18
8. ( ) C#3 and G#3	G#	10	28
9. ( ) G#2 and D#3	D#	7	21
10. ( ) D#3 and A#3	A#	11	31
11. ( ) A#2 and F3	F	8	24
12. ( ) F2 and C3	Check only.	6*	18*

NOTE: Step #12 is a check of how accurately the tuning was performed. If the indicated number of beats are heard in this check, the Organ is in perfect tune. If the beats counted are within ±3 beats of the indicated beats, it is acceptable. The number of beats that you hear above or below the indicated beats represents the total tuning error accumulated during fine adjustment of the eleven coils.

* ±3 beats are acceptable on this check. If more or less, repeat all the above steps.

Courtesy Heath Co.

Chart 4-2. Fine Tuning Chart

tuning procedure. In this example, the tool is turned 1¾ turns clockwise.

7. Repeat Step 5, this time tuning the A# oscillator while using the newly tuned B oscillator as reference. That is, B2 and A#2 are played simultaneously, and the A# oscillator is adjusted for zero beat.

8. Rough tuning of the A# oscillator is then accomplished by turning the slug in the A# coil clockwise. In this example, the slug is turned 2¼ turns clockwise.

9. The remainder of the oscillators are rough-tuned in a similar manner. In this example, the slugs are turned by the amounts tabulated in Chart 4-1.

In most cases, the foregoing rough-tuning procedure will be followed by a fine-tuning schedule. The trombone voice is utilized instead of the flute voice. Adjustments are made on the basis of counting beats over a given time interval, such as 10 seconds. If the oscillators are reasonably close to correct tuning, their operating frequencies will be on the correct side of zero beat. In case of doubt, return a slug to its zero-beat position, and then rotate the slug clockwise until a stipulated number of beats are counted in a 10-second interval. For maximum accuracy, count beats over a 30-second interval, as tabulated in Chart 4-2. A watch with a second hand is required, and the alignment tool should always be removed from a coil before starting to count beats.

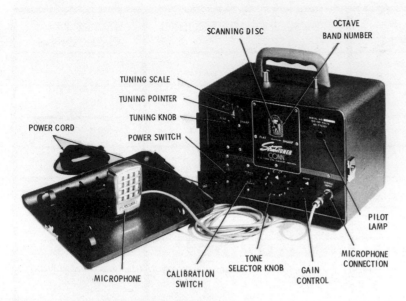

SCANNING DISC
OCTAVE BAND NUMBER
TUNING SCALE
TUNING POINTER
TUNING KNOB
POWER CORD
POWER SWITCH
PILOT LAMP
MICROPHONE CONNECTION
MICROPHONE
CALIBRATION SWITCH
TONE SELECTOR KNOB
GAIN CONTROL

Fig. 4-15. The Conn *Strobotuner*.

Fig. 4-16. The *Strobotuner* disc.

The beat method is classic, and applies to any organ, regardless of the tone-generator design.

Although comparatively expensive, a set of tuning forks can be purchased, and each oscillator can be tuned directly against a standard reference pitch. However, the beat method is highly precise when followed conscientiously, and only one fork is required. Various electrical and electronic tuning aids have also been devised, and are preferred by some technicians. A tuning aid usually permits appreciable saving of time, and is less tedious than counting beats. The first electronic tuning aid was the Conn *Strobotuner,* illustrated in Fig. 4-15. It operates on a stroboscopic principle, as do most other designs. It employs a rotating disc with a strobe pattern, as seen in Fig. 4-16. Operating details are not presented in this book, since tuning aids are provided with complete instruction manuals. Before starting to tune the tone generators in any organ, always consult the organ service manual, regardless of the tuning method that may be preferred. This work habit can save considerable time that otherwise may be wasted by making false starts.

Chapter 5

Servicing the Keying System

There is no sharp dividing line between simple keyswitch arrangements and elaborate configurations employing electronic-switch networks that may also perform automatic sequential circuit actions. However, it is helpful to form general categories based on increasing orders of complexity. Within any category, such as mechanical switching devices, various subgroups will be encountered. Efficient troubleshooting requires that the operation of a keying system be clearly understood, so that logical signal-tracing procedures can be followed, and voltage measurements can be evaluated. Therefore, the following section explains the typical circuits, devices, and systems that are encountered in this area.

SWITCHING ARRANGEMENTS AND IDENTIFICATION

Basic mechanical keyswitches were explained previously. A typical elaboration of the mechanical system is shown in Fig. 5-1. This is called a coupler arrangement, and permits one to play tones on one manual by depressing keys on another manual; couplers may also provide for the simultaneous sounding of octavely related tones on the same manual, when an individual key is depressed. A coupler is turned *on* or *off* by means of a stop tablet. In the example of Fig. 5-1, the coupler rods are rotated into their *on* or *off* positions by means of stop tablets. In turn, the key-contact fingers wil make and break the 75-volt circuit in the *on* position, but are insulated from the 75-volt bus in the *off* position, as shown in Fig. 5-2. Trouble symptoms have the same causes as in simple keying arrangements—contacts tend to collect foreign matter such as lint or dust with the passage of time.

Case histories have noted trouble due to contact damage caused by attempted cleaning with coarse abrasives. Contact fingers are comparatively thin, and may be bent to one side if accidentally bumped by a tool or flashlight. If a trouble symptom is due to mechanical damage, it is often advisable to replace the assembly. As noted previously, keyswitch adjustments are generally provided. A switch should be adjusted so that the note starts to sound when the key is approximately halfway down. In this example, the time of contact is determined by a metal tab that contacts the keyswitch post toward the front of the key channel. This tab can be bent up or down slightly, as required. Another metal tab toward the rear of the key channel determines the tension of the key spring. It is normally adjusted for a tension of 3 ounces.

ELECTRONIC SWITCHING

Various types of electronic switches are used in organs for keying and gating. These terms are sometimes used interchangeably. However, keying denotes a direct response to a manual act, whereas gating denotes a timed and automatic response that is triggered by a preceding response. Solid-state devices are widely used for switching and gating. Neon tubes will be found in some older-model organs. Light-dependent resistors (LDRs) have also been employed. Fig. 5-3 depicts a basic diode-keying cir-

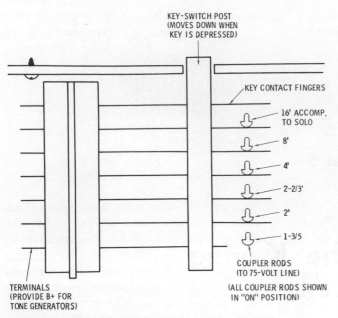

Fig. 5-1. Mechanical keying arrangement with coupler rods.

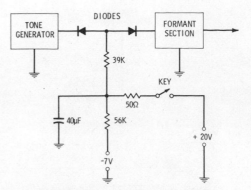

Fig. 5-3. Basic diode keying circuit.

cuit. It controls the flow of audio signal from the tone generator to the formant section. A pair of diodes connected back-to-back are inserted in series with the lead from the tone generator to the formant section. When the key is open, both diodes are cut off (reverse biased) by the −7-volt source. Therefore, the output from the tone generator is blocked. On the other hand, when the key is closed, the +20-volt source overrides the −7-volt source, and both diodes become conducting (forward biased). In turn, the output signal from the tone generator is applied to the formant section. Note that the 40-μF capacitor is a waveshaping component; it is considered in detail in the chapter on voicing.

A basic transistor keying circuit is shown in Fig. 5-4. The circuit action is similar to that of the diode configuration described previously. Note that the output from the tone generator is applied to the emitter, and the output load circuit is connected to the collector. Bias voltages are applied to the base of the transistor to control the switching action. When the key is open, a negative voltage is fed to the base of the npn transistor through the 2.2-megohm resistor. Thus, the transistor is biased beyond collector-current cutoff. On the other hand, when the key is closed, a positive bias voltage overrides the negative

bias voltage via the 68k-ohm resistor. In turn, the transistor conducts, and operates as a common-base amplifier. Transistor keying circuits are often associated with diode-keying circuits in the more elaborate configurations. Details are described subsequently.

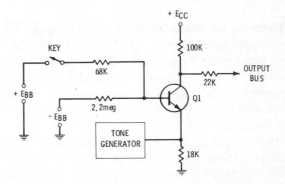

Fig. 5-4. Basic transistor keying circuit.

Fig. 5-5 shows a basic neon-bulb switching arrangement. A neon bulb is practically an open circuit until a certain voltage value, called the *breakdown potential*, is applied across the bulb. The bulb then glows and its internal resistance suddenly falls to a comparatively low value. If the potential drop across the bulb is reduced sufficiently, the *extinction potential* will be reached, whereupon the bulb suddenly stops glowing and becomes practically an open circuit once more. The voltage-current characteristic for a neon bulb is shown in Fig. 5-5B. As the applied voltage is increased from A to B, the bulb "strikes" at B, and quickly assumes its steady "on" state at C. Note that there is a small amount of current (typically 1 μA) prior to B; this is called the dark current, and is so small that it can be disregarded in switching circuits. Over the normal operating range from C to D, the voltage drop across the bulb remains almost constant, although the current increases rapidly. From D to E, the bulb becomes overloaded, and will be damaged at current levels

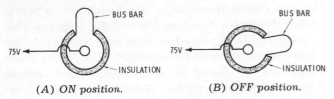

(A) ON position.   (B) OFF position.

Fig. 5-2. End view of coupler rod.

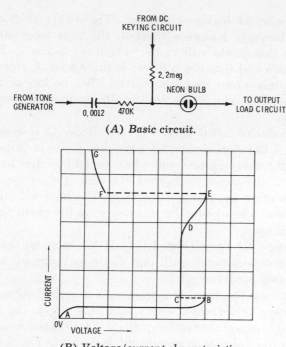

(A) Basic circuit.

(B) Voltage/current characteristic.

Fig. 5-5. Neon-bulb switching arrangement.

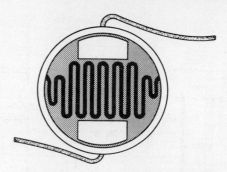

Fig. 5-7. Appearance of an LDR.

higher than E. Note that if the voltage drop across the bulb is removed, the path of operation will return quickly to A.

Light-dependent resistors, also called photoconductive cell-lamps, are used in switching circuits, particularly when an attenuating function is also required. That is, when the illumination level is increased, the internal resistance of a light-dependent resistor (LDR) may vary from practically an open circuit to a value of 100 ohms, or less. Accordingly, reliable control of volume is provided in addition to

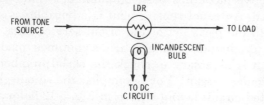

Fig. 5-6. LDR operating as switch and attenuator.

switching action. One of the useful elaborations of the basic design entails the control of a number of tone circuits by means of a single incandescent bulb. LDRs are usually of the cadmium-sulfide or cadmium-selenide types. A typical LDR is seen in Fig. 5-7.

Diode keying may be combined with neon-bulb switching, as in the example of Fig. 5-8. In this example, the diodes are connected series-aiding, and the keying voltage is applied through a 1-megohm resistor to the left-hand diode. The keying-voltage

source has a value of −100 volts, and causes both diodes to conduct when the key is closed. Closure of the key also causes the 0.47-μF capacitor to charge, so that the diodes do not stop conducting immediately when the key is opened. The time constant of this circuit is approximately one-half second; this is an aspect of voicing, as described in greater detail in the following chapter. When a short time constant is desired, the switch to the +80-volt source is closed, and the neon bulb conducts. In turn, when the key is opened, the 0.47-μF capacitor discharges rapidly (about four times as fast).

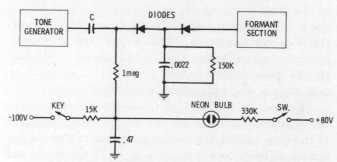

Fig. 5-8. Combined diode and neon-bulb switching.

Transistor keying is often combined with diode switching, as shown in Fig. 5-9. In this example, a small fixed negative bias is applied to the base of the transistor. Thus, the transistor is cut off until the key is depressed. When the circuit is keyed on, the positive voltage overrides the negative bias voltage at the base of the transistor, causing collector current. In turn, the signal from the tone generator, which is applied to the emitter, is amplified at the collector. The transistor operates as a common-base amplifier. When the key is opened, the positive charge on the 0.47-μF capacitor decays slowly through the 2.2-megohm resistor. This is an aspect of voicing action. In case a fast discharge is desired, a negative voltage, instead of a positive voltage, is applied to the cathode of the diode. Therefore, the positive charge on the 0.47-μF capacitor discharges rapidly via the diode.

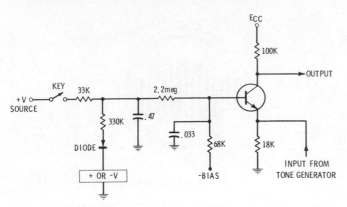

Fig. 5-9. Combined transistor and diode switching.

TROUBLES IN SEMICONDUCTOR SWITCHING CIRCUITS

Some practical examples of trouble symptoms and their cures in the keying system of an organ will now be considered. With reference to the block diagram shown in Fig. 5-10, a +12-volt supply energizes the solo key contacts, the Great key contacts, the accompaniment key contacts, and the pedal key contacts. From the main tone generator, an ac signal is fed to the 8′ solo signal keyer, the piano signal keyer, the 8′ Great signal keyer, the 16′ Great signal keyer, the 4′ accompaniment signal keyer, the 8′ accompaniment signal keyer, the 8′ pedal signal keyer, and the 16′ pedal signal keyer. It is helpful to start by considering the tibia keyer circuitry.

As shown in Fig. 5-11, the tibia generator is keyed through double diode keyers. In the "off" condition of the stop switch, the switching bus is at ground potential. When a key is depressed, +12 volts is applied to the keyer at resistor R1. Switching diode X1 conducts and shorts the keying voltage to ground. R1 serves as a current-limiting resistor. Because X1 provides practically a short-circuit to ground through Q1, no current is conducted by X2. On the other hand, in the "on" condition of the stop switch, transistor Q1 is cut off, and the collector is not at ground potential. Therefore, when the key is depressed, +12 volts is applied to X2, and there is current through X2 to the oscillator. We will recall that organs are generally designed so that the manual keys are "dead" until a stop switch is closed. Trouble symptoms are associated with component defects, as follows:

Transistor Q1 shorted (Fig. 5-11): It is evident that in case Q1 becomes shorted, closure of the stop switch will not cause the collector to float free from ground. The trouble symptom is failure of the diode keyer to turn on when the associated tab is turned on.

Diode X1 leaky or shorted (Fig. 5-11): If diode X1 becomes leaky or shorted, the note associated with that diode will cipher whenever a key is depressed and that diode keyer is turned on. A cipher is simply a tone that is produced when no key is depressed. Diode X1 is technically termed a clamp diode.

Diode X2 leaky (Fig. 5-11): If diode X2 is leaky, and if the stop associated with that diode is turned off, the note will be weak when keyed by other keyers. If the diode is shorted, the note (when keyed from other keyers) will be dead. The note will also be dead when keyed by this keyer, in the event that X2 is open.

Diode X1 open (Fig. 5-11): If X1 becomes open, the note associated with that diode will play even if the stop is turned off.

In case the trouble symptom is a cipher when a solo key is depressed and a solo tibia stop is on, we would suspect that a clamp diode is leaky, and would seek to localize it in the circuitry shown in Fig. 5-11. In this example, printed circuitry is employed, and we would consult the service manual, to find the layout shown in Fig. 5-12. If either of the diodes shown in heavy outlines is leaky, a single constant note will be heard in the background when almost any key is depressed.

The leaky diode in this example can be located best by using a test lead as a probe. If a VOM is set on a high-current range, and one lead is connected to ground, the other lead will serve as a convenient probe. When the probe is contacted with the terminal of the leaky diode, the leakage current is thereby shorted to ground and the cipher will stop. After the defective diode has been pinpointed, it must be replaced. An exact replacement is advisable, as specified in the parts list of the organ service data. Note that production changes are sometimes made, so that it is necessary to check the serial number of a particular organ. For example, the diode keyer printed-circuit layout shown in Fig. 5-12 is for a late production run; the early production run used the diode keyer printed-circuit layout shown in Fig. 5-13.

Next, let us consider the signal keyers represented in the block diagram of Fig. 5-10. In this example, each keyer comprises three diodes, as shown in Fig. 5-14. These keyers operate from a +12-volt source. Note that the signal source is the main generator, which produces a square-wave signal. This is a dc square wave, so that the waveform is grounded for one-half of its period, and has a peak value of +12 volts for the other half of its period. Signal-keyer diode X2 will not conduct unless its oscillator end is negative with respect to its other end. With no key

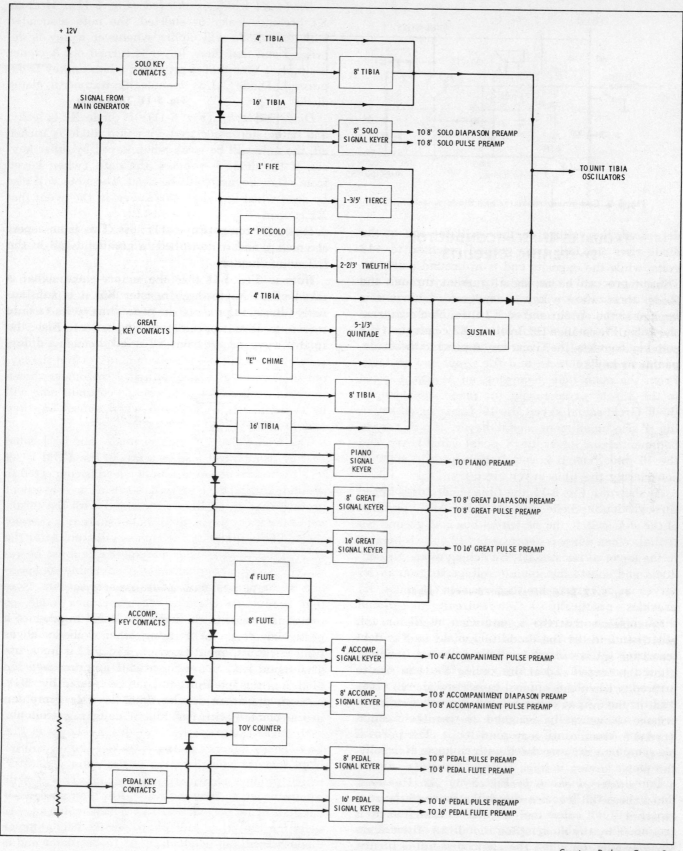

Courtesy Rodgers Organ Co.

Fig. 5-10. Block diagram of keyer circuits.

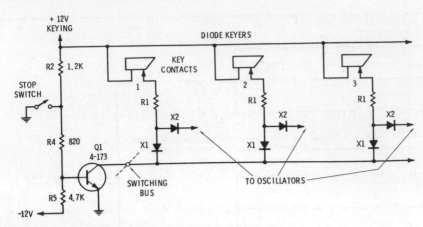

Fig. 5-11. Tibia keyer.

depressed, the voltage on the oscillator end of the diode rises and falls from ground potential to +12 volts, while the opposite end is at ground potential. Thus, there can be no signal current through the diode. Next, when a key is depressed, +12 volts is applied to the output end of X2 through a comparatively high resistance R2. In turn, X2 conducts. (If a pedal is depressed, +7 volts are applied to the diode, in this example.)

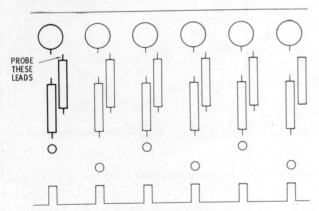

Fig. 5-12. Diode keyer printed-circuit layout.

We observe that the square-wave oscillator will pull both ends of the diode to ground in Fig. 5-14 when the square wave has zero potential, and will allow the output end of the keying diode to rise to +12 volts when the square wave rises to +12 volts. That is, the output voltage of X2 duplicates its input voltage. Now, let us consider the pedal ff action (pedal fortissimo, or very loud tone). The pedal ff operates by changing the keying voltage. Normally, the pedal keying voltage is only 4 volts, so that a 4-volt square wave is processed by X2. However, when the pedal ff is depressed, the keying voltage is changed to 7 volts, and a 7-volt square wave is processed by the diode. (See Fig. 5-15.) The voltage waveform on the keyer rises with moderate rapidity, holds constant until the keyer is released, and then

decays with comparative slowness. This is an aspect of voicing, and is described in greater detail in the following chapter.

Note in Fig. 5-14 that the square-wave signal is taken off at X2 through resistor R5; it is substantially filtered to produce the pedal flute tones (a flute waveform is an approximate sine wave). Also, the square-wave output from X2 is fed through a differ-

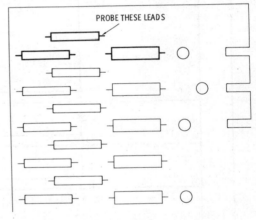

Fig. 5-13. Diode printed-circuit layout.

entiating circuit C3R4 and a diode X4 to produce a pulse waveform for forming other voices such as tibia mirabilis, open diapason, and viol d'orchestra. The signal keyers are fabricated as printed-circuit boards in this example, and can be located by reference to the organ service data. Trouble symptoms are associated with component defects, as follows:

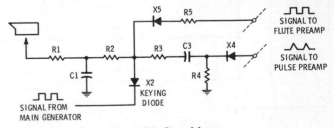

Fig. 5-14. Signal keyer.

Diode X2 shorted or leaky (Fig. 5-14): If X2 becomes shorted or leaky, the note associated with that diode will cipher whenever one of the main-generator stops is turned on.

Diode X2 open (Fig. 5-14): If diode X2 is open, the associated note will be dead.

Diode X4 shorted (Fig. 5-14): If X4 is shorted, the tonal quality of the associated note will be abnormal, except on the flute voice.

Diode X4 open (Fig. 5-14): If X4 is open, the associated note will be dead except on the flute voice.

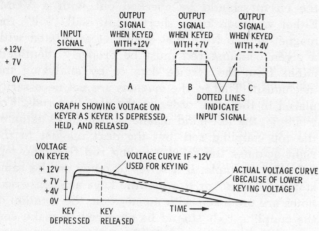

Fig. 5-15. Signal keyer waveforms.

In case the trouble symptom in this example is a continuous cipher when a Great stop is on (other than a tibia stop), we will suspect a leaky diode in the Great signal keyer. After the pertinent PC board has been located, the leaky diode can be pinpointed conveniently by using a test lead as a probe (refer to previous discussion of Fig. 5-11). When the probe contacts a leaky diode terminal (Fig. 5-16), the signal is thereby shorted to ground, and the cipher will stop. In turn, the defective diode is replaced. It is advisable to use an exact replacement type of diode. With reference to Fig. 5-14, it is evi-

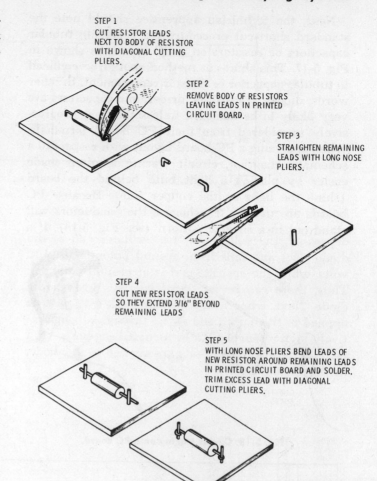

STEP 1
CUT RESISTOR LEADS NEXT TO BODY OF RESISTOR WITH DIAGONAL CUTTING PLIERS.

STEP 2
REMOVE BODY OF RESISTORS LEAVING LEADS IN PRINTED CIRCUIT BOARD.

STEP 3
STRAIGHTEN REMAINING LEADS WITH LONG NOSE PLIERS.

STEP 4
CUT NEW RESISTOR LEADS SO THEY EXTEND 3/16" BEYOND REMAINING LEADS

STEP 5
WITH LONG NOSE PLIERS BEND LEADS OF NEW RESISTOR AROUND REMAINING LEADS IN PRINTED CIRCUIT BOARD AND SOLDER. TRIM EXCESS LEAD WITH DIAGONAL CUTTING PLIERS.

Fig. 5-17. Short-cut method of replacing tubular capacitors and resistors.

dent that a trouble symptom such as a dead note on all voices but the flute voice could be caused by capacitor C3 opening up, as well as by an open in X4. Therefore, when more than one fault may be present in a signal-keyer circuit, time can often be saved by signal-tracing with a scope.

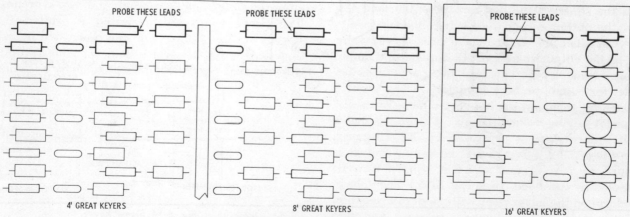

Fig. 5-16. Keying diodes are indicated by heavy lines.

Next, the technician apprentice should note the standard short-cut procedure for replacing tubular capacitors or resistors on a PC board, as shown in Fig. 5-17. This short-cut method should be confined to tubular capacitor or resistor replacement. In other words, diodes, transistors, or ceramic capacitors are very likely to be damaged unless they are progressively unsoldered from their PC board terminals. When analyzing a PC-board layout with respect to a schematic diagram, circuit tracing is often made easier by placing a light bulb behind the board (shine the light on the copper side). Because PC boards are usually translucent, the conductors will stand out in a shadow pattern (see Fig. 5-18). If a

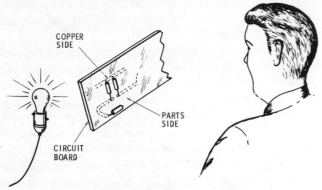

Fig. 5-18. Circuit tracing on a PC board.

trouble lamp is not available, a good flashlight will serve the purpose.

COUPLER TROUBLESHOOTING

When mechanical switches are employed in coupler keying systems, as shown in Figs. 5-1 and 5-2, the coupling rods may be rotated by actuating electromagnets, as exemplified in Fig. 5-19. Approximately 13 volts is applied to a magnet coil via the associated stop tab. If a magnet becomes inoperative, the circuit should be checked out with a VOM. Either an open or a short-circuit will "kill" the magnet action. Note that a magnet associated with a given coupling rod must be properly identified, either from the service data or by analyzing the mechanism. That is, the magnets are not necessarily placed in the same order as the coupling rods. For example, the left-hand magnet in Fig. 5-19 actuates the top coupling rod, but the next magnet to the right actuates the third coupling rod from the top.

In this example, if a series of notes on the same stop are "dead," or if, when the keys are depressed, notes are produced with no stops on, the rotation of the coupling rods should be observed to make certain that the "on" and "off" positions are normal. For example, in Fig. 5-19, rod 410A is shown in the

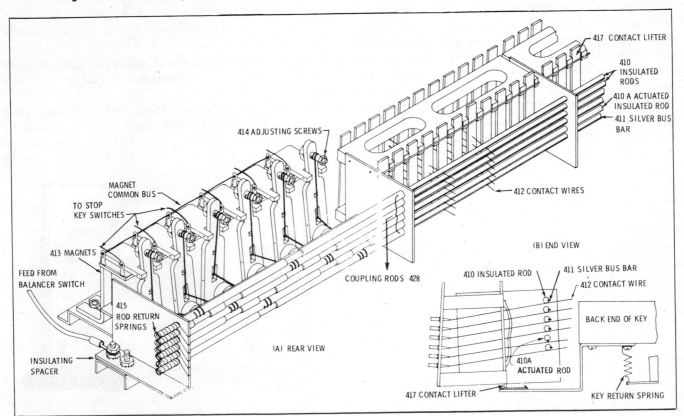

Fig. 5-19. Keyswitch assembly.

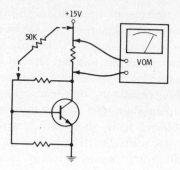

Fig. 5-21. Turn-on test of a transistor.

"on" position, and rods 410 are shown in the "off" position. Note adjusting screws 414; if the position of a rod is incorrect, the adjusting screw should be turned as required. This adjustment should be made for the "on" position, since the "off" position is not particularly critical. If a rod does not return to its "off" position, the associated return spring may be defective. Springs 415 must be sufficiently strong to rotate the rod normally, but must not prevent the magnet from pulling the rod in. Since the actuating voltage tends to decrease under load, a test should be made with all the other magnets on. To adjust spring tension in this example, the spring is pulled out of its retaining slot, given one-half turn in the required direction, and returned to the slot.

"TURN-OFF" AND "TURN-ON" TRANSISTOR TESTING

Technicians often use quick-checks when it is practical to do so, to minimize testing time. For example, a turn-off test of a transistor, as given in Fig. 5-20, is often useful. In this example, we may assume that the transistor is conducting, as indicated by a near-zero collector-voltage indication. To determine whether the transistor has normal control action, it is only necessary to short-circuit the base and emitter terminals. The short circuit brings the base and emitter to the same potential (in this example, to ground potential). Therefore, the transistor will go into collector-current cutoff, unless it is defective. Cutoff is indicated by a jump of the voltmeter reading up to the value of the collector supply voltage; in this example, the collector voltage will jump up to 12 volts if the transistor has normal control action.

In other configurations, a turn-off test is not practical. For example, if the base and emitter are short-circuited in the circuit of Fig. 5-21, an appreciable and unknown value of current is drawn from the collector electrode through the short circuit; therefore, it becomes impractical to evaluate the test results. However, considerable useful information can be obtained concerning the condition of the transistor by means of a turn-on test. To make a turn-on test,

connect the voltmeter across the collector load resistor, and bleed supply voltage into the base through a 50k-ohm resistor, as indicated. If the meter reading increases substantially, the transistor has normal amplifying action.

Most defective transistors can be pinpointed in-circuit by means of terminal-voltage measurements. However, in case the normal terminal voltages are not specified in the organ service data, turn-off and turn-on tests can be very helpful. Although in-circuit transistor testers are available, organ technicians usually prefer out-of-circuit testers, such as the one illustrated in Fig. 5-22. The reason for reduced utility of in-circuit testers in organ servicing is the incidence of somewhat unusual transistor circuitry, as noted previously in examples where a transistor may be connected to several diodes. The instrument in Fig. 5-22 provides measurements of transistor beta and collector leakage current. These are the fundamental parameters of concern in service tests of transistors.

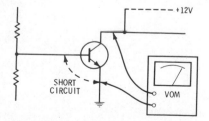

Fig. 5-20. Turn-off test of a transistor.

Courtesy Triplett Electrical Instrument Co.

Fig. 5-22. A typical transistor tester.

Chapter 6

Troubles in the Voicing Section

Voicing denotes a resultant tone output obtained by production of a specified distribution of overtones with respect to a certain pitch. From the viewpoint of waveform analysis, voicing signifies a complex output waveform produced by a specified array of harmonics that have various required amplitudes with respect to the fundamental. As noted previously, voicing is often concerned with phase relations between two or more pitches (fundamental frequencies). Recall also that voicing entails the rise time and fall time (attack and sustain characteristics) of a waveform. It has been mentioned that voicing processes may include amplitude modulation, frequency modulation, or phase modulation (from a practical point of view the latter can be regarded as a form of frequency modulation). With these basic facts in mind, the technician is in a good position to consider troubleshooting procedures in voicing sections of electronic organs.

VOICING CIRCUIT ACTION

All voicing circuits are waveshapers, and the majority have filter action. Typical voicing filters are shown in Fig. 6-1. Voicing filters are also called formant filters, tone changers, or simply formants. The simplest configurations are RC differentiating or integrating circuits, or elaborations thereof. Fig. 6-2 typifies the next step in complexity, which involves RCL networks. Filter networks have been mounted in shield cans with plug bases, to facilitate replacement in case that a component defect occurs. However, there has been a trend toward fabrication on printed-circuit boards, or as packaged electronic circuits. These designs also facilitate replacement, and minimize down-time for the customer.

A packaged circuit is illustrated in Fig. 6-3. This is an RC configuration; when inductors are used, they are separate from packaged circuits. Although a printed circuit can be repaired by replacement of defective components, a packaged circuit must be discarded if it becomes defective. Fig. 6-4 shows a representative configuration for a printed-circuit voicing or formant filter. A formant-filter system is sometimes called a quality-control section, as in the example of Fig. 6-5. In any case, the terminology is descriptive, and the general location of the filters can be determined from block diagrams and pictorial diagrams provided in service manuals. The scope is the most useful type of signal tracer in a filter system, in order to close in on a defective component. Trouble symptoms range from a "dead" voice to weak and/or distorted voices. In any case, we are concerned with the presence or absence, and with the shapes and amplitudes of the various waveforms.

Although filter action and filter characteristics are not entirely simple, there are various basic principles that are helpful to keep in mind when analyzing trouble symptoms. Single- and multiple-section integrating circuits are often used in formant filters. Fig. 6-6 shows the waveshaping action that is involved, with comparative rise times and leading edges for one-, two-, and three-section configurations. These data are presented in the form of a universal time-constant chart, and apply to all symmetrical integrating circuits. A symmetrical circuit

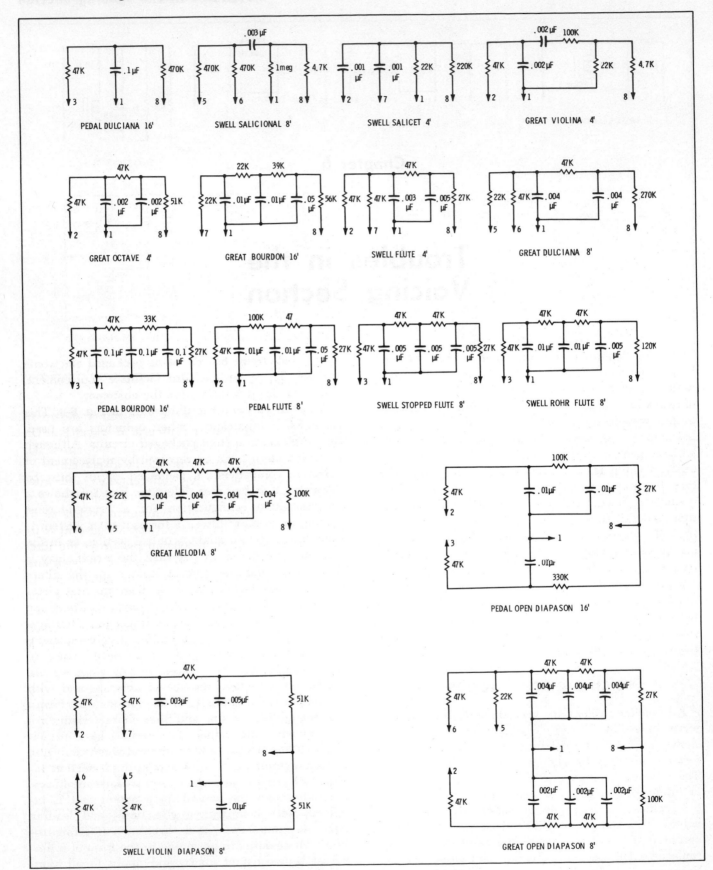

Fig. 6-1. Typical voicing filters of the RC type.

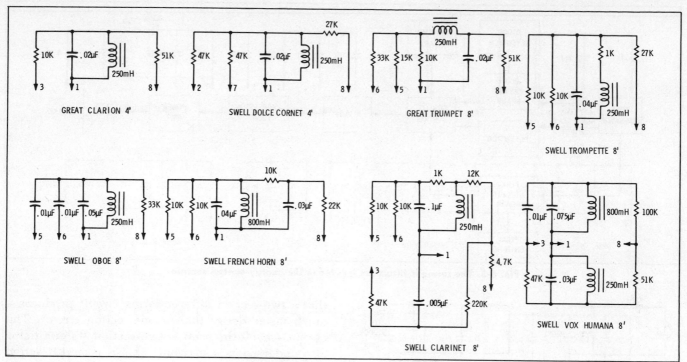

Fig. 6-2. Typical voicing filters of the RCL type.

is one that employs the same values of R and C in each section. In Fig. 6-6E, we observe that the output waveform falls in the same time and in the same manner as it rises. The technical description of equal rise and fall times is equal attack and decay, or equal attack and sustain times.

When multiple-section integrating circuits are unsymmetrical, the general nature of the response is the same as for symmetrical circuits. However, the leading and trailing edges will not have the same timing, nor quite the same shape as in the symmetrical situation. Single- and multiple-section differentiating circuits are also utilized in formant filters. In a simple RC series circuit, a differentiated waveform appears across the resistor, and an integrated waveform appears across the capacitor, as shown in

Figs. 6-7A and B. The scope connection shown in Fig. 6-7C will display the integrated waveform. On the other hand, if the scope is connected across R1, the differentiated waveform will be displayed.

Note in Fig. 6-7B that differentiated and integrated waveforms are the reverse of each other. For example, the differentiated waveform decays to 37 percent of its peak amplitude (loses 63 percent of its amplitude) in one time-constant, whereas the integrated waveform rises to 37 percent of its peak amplitude (acquires 63 percent of its amplitude) in one time-constant. Another way of describing this relationship is to state that the differentiated waveform is the same as the integrated waveform "turned upside down." Next, we observe in Figs. 6-7D and E

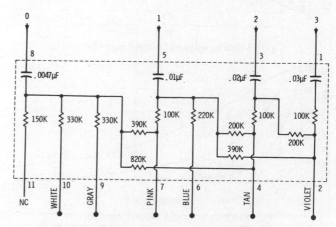

Fig. 6-3. A packaged unit.

Fig. 6-4. Configuration of a typical PC voicing filter.

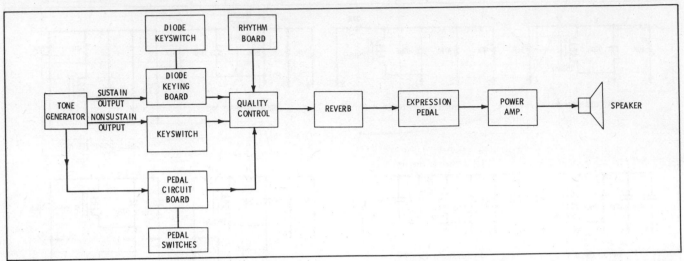

Fig. 6-5. The formant filters are located in the quality-control section.

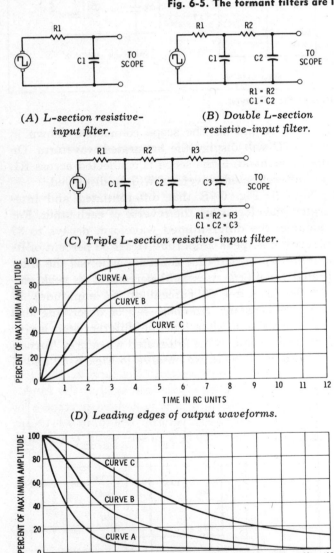

(A) *L-section resistive-input filter.*

(B) *Double L-section resistive-input filter.*

(C) *Triple L-section resistive-input filter.*

(D) *Leading edges of output waveforms.*

(E) *Trailing edges of output waveforms.*

Fig. 6-6. Examples of L-section filters.

that a two-section differentiating circuit produces a much faster decay than a one-section circuit. The output waveform from a two-section differentiator also undershoots somewhat—this is a circuit action that is more often encountered in RLC circuits. Note in passing that it can be shown that a two-section RC differentiating circuit has an equivalent series RLC circuit.

All simple RC circuits have equivalent RL circuits. For example, Fig. 6-8 shows a universal RL time-constant chart for RL differentiating and integrating circuits. A comparison with the universal time-constant chart for RC differentiating and integrating circuits, shown in Fig. 6-7B, reveals identical curves, with the only distinction that time is measured in RC units instead of L/R units. Therefore, it follows that the RC and RL circuits shown in Fig. 6-9 are equivalent. This fact follows from the simple equation $RC = L/R$; solving for L, we obtain $L = R^2C$. Note that if the inductance has a large value, the output waveform may differ from the waveform predicted by simple theory because a large inductor has appreciable distributed capacitance. In turn, the inductor does not respond practically as an ideal inductor; instead, the large inductor responds as a self-resonant circuit. This type of response may be required in particular formants; examples are seen in Fig. 6-2.

Any filter has a certain frequency response, as well as a certain transient response. For example, Fig. 6-10 shows the universal frequency-response chart for an RC differentiating circuit. Beginners should be careful to avoid confusion between transient-response curves and frequency-response curves. In other words, the curves shown in Fig. 6-7B are transient-response curves and indicate the out-

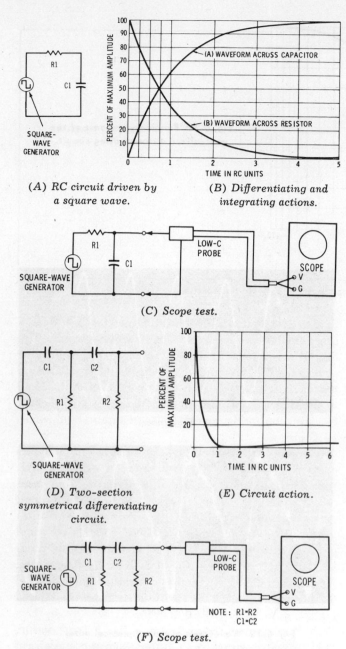

(A) *RC circuit driven by a square wave.*

(B) *Differentiating and integrating actions.*

(C) *Scope test.*

(D) *Two-section symmetrical differentiating circuit.*

(E) *Circuit action.*

(F) *Scope test.*

Fig. 6-7. Differentiating circuits and characteristics.

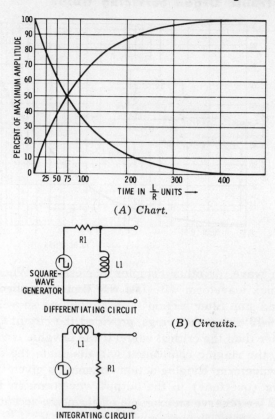

(A) *Chart.*

(B) *Circuits.*

Fig. 6-8. Universal RL time-constant chart.

put voltage that results from application of a square-wave voltage to the input terminals. On the other hand, the curve shown in Fig. 6-10 shows the sine-wave output of the circuit versus frequency. Note that the transient response of a filter is related to its frequency response; however, the calculations are so involved that the practical technician makes use of transient-response and frequency-response charts. Fig. 6-11 shows a universal frequency response chart for a single-section integrating circuit. In scope checks of circuit action, we are usually concerned with waveforms and amplitudes. Fig. 6-12 illustrates waveshapes for flute and horn notes. If a particular

waveform and amplitude are not specified in the organ service data, it may be possible to make a comparison test on a similar organ that is in good operating condition.

As noted previously, filter configurations of the general type shown in Fig. 6-2 make use of the resonant response of LC circuits. The most usual arrangement is a parallel-resonant circuit connected in series with the signal lead, as indicated in Fig. 6-13A. This is a basic band-stop network, and it provides the frequency characteristic shown in Fig. 6-13B. In some applications, the resonant frequency f_o is designed to coincide with the fundamental frequency of a complex waveform, so that the fundamental is substantially attenuated with respect to the harmonics of the waveform. The input waveform to a formant filter may be a square wave, pulse, saw-

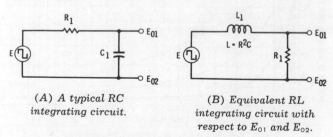

(A) *A typical RC integrating circuit.*

(B) *Equivalent RL integrating circuit with respect to E_{01} and E_{02}.*

Fig. 6-9. An RC circuit can be equivalent to an RL circuit.

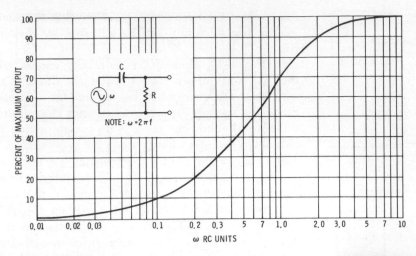

Fig. 6-10. Frequency response of the generalized differentiating circuit.

tooth wave, or other complex waveshape. When a complex waveform with fast rise time is applied to a band-stop filter section such as the one shown in Fig. 6-13, the circuit rings, provided the circuit Q is greater than the critical value. If the Q value is very high, the ringing component will dominate the output waveform. Ringing action enhances a given harmonic (overtone) in the output waveform; in Fig. 6-12B we observe an example of harmonic accentuation in a semisawtooth waveform.

When a distorted, weak, or otherwise abnormal waveform is displayed at the output of a formant filter, the input waveform should be checked next as a matter of routine. If the input waveform is normal, we know that the trouble will be found in the filter section. Statistically, capacitors are the most common troublemakers. The next most likely fault is a poor connection, such as a cold-soldered joint. Since filter inductors are often wound with very fine wire, we may find an open coil due to previous excessive current drain, corrosion, or mechanical damage. Sometimes a printed-circuit conductor becomes cracked or broken, with the result that operation

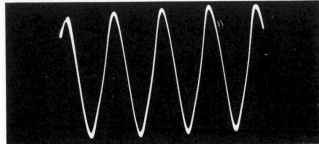

(A) Flute note.

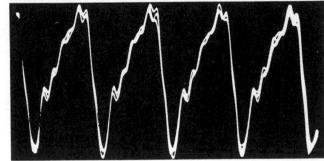

(B) Horn note.

Fig. 6-12. Waveforms of typical musical notes.

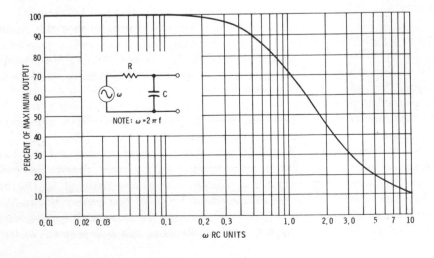

Fig. 6-11. Frequency response of the generalized integrating circuit.

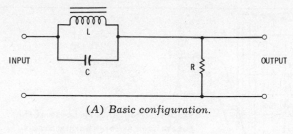

(A) *Basic configuration.*

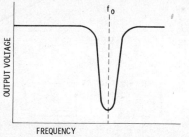

(B) *Frequency response.*

Fig. 6-13. LCR bandstop filter.

stops or is intermittent. Signal-tracing tests are most useful in pinpointing a defective PC conductor. In many cases, the defect can be repaired by "jumping" the PC conductor with a piece of hookup wire soldered at each end of the printed conductor.

SUSTAIN VOICING CIRCUITS AND TROUBLES

It was noted earlier that a sustained tone is produced by a waveform that has a comparatively slow decay. For example, the waveform of a typical sustained tone is displayed on the scope screen as shown in Fig. 6-14. Depending upon the voice that is in use, the decay interval may be normally longer or shorter. We will often find that a large capacitor is used to provide sustain action, as exemplified in Fig. 6-15. The capacitor is connected between the

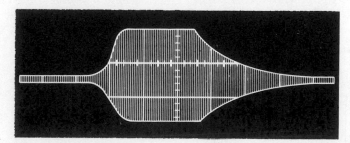

Fig. 6-14. Waveform of a typical sustained tone.

oscillator keying lead and ground. When a key is depressed, dc voltage is applied to the oscillator and to the sustain capacitor. Next, when the key is released, the sustain capacitor slowly discharges into the oscillator section. As the voltage decays, the

loudness of the tone decreases. Note that the sustain length (decay time) can be adjusted by means of R6.

In Fig. 6-15, diode X2 is normally connected to the +12 volt supply via R4. Thus, the diode is normally cut off, even when keying voltage is present. Since the sustain capacitor C2 cannot charge under this circuit condition, there is no sustain action provided. On the other hand, when X2 is grounded, the sustain capacitor is effectively grounded because it can then charge through X2 and discharge through X3, thereby providing sustain action. In this example, the tibia sustain stop tab turns on the short-sustain function by grounding R6 instead of diode X2. In this situation, the sustain capacitor can charge only to the voltage permitted by R4. When the key is released, the circuit voltage drops to this value, and the sustain action proceeds from this level. Note that potentiometer R6 determines this starting level, and in turn the length of the sustain action. The ref-

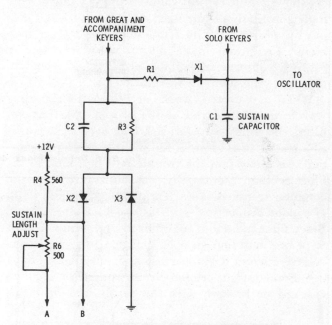

Fig. 6-15. A sustain voicing configuration.

erence sustain length is determined by the value of R3. Diode X1 is an isolating diode; it functions to isolate the sustain action so that the tibia voices on the solo manual can be played normally even when Great and accompaniment tibia voices are played with sustain action.

Fig. 6-16 presents the short-sustain and the long-sustain circuit actions in greater detail. Basically, the circuit time-constants are changed in the two modes of operation. Next, with reference to Fig. 6-15, R6 is grounded through a contact-multiplying diode (Fig. 6-17) when the harp tab is depressed. In turn,

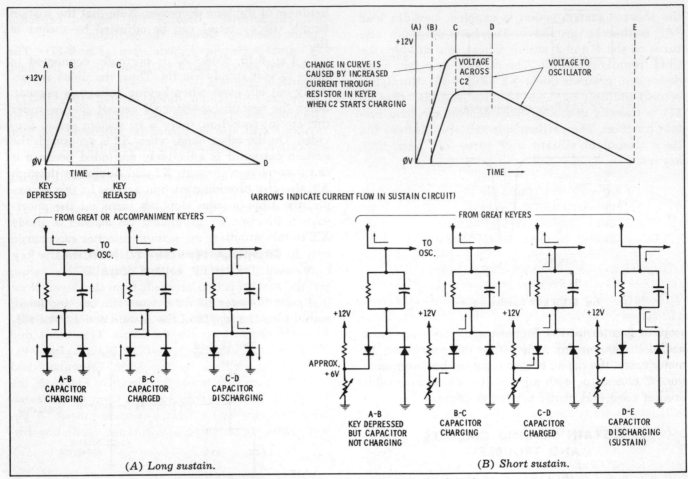

(A) Long sustain.   (B) Short sustain.

Fig. 6-16. Details of long- and short-sustain circuit actions.

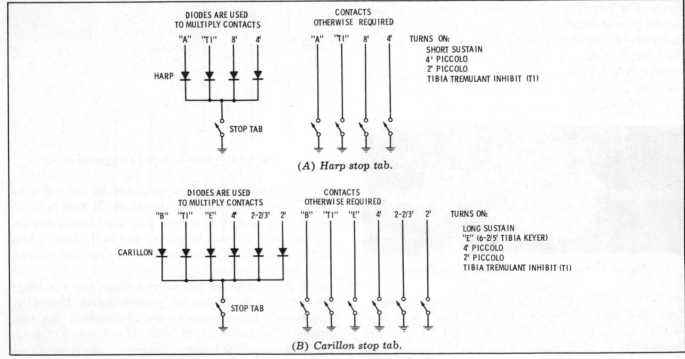

(A) Harp stop tab.

(B) Carillon stop tab.

Fig. 6-17. Contact-multiplying diode circuits.

the short-sustain function is enabled, because lead "A" is thereby grounded. The harp stop tab also turns on the 4' and 2' piccolo voices, and disables the tibia tremulant/vibrato. The carillon stop tab, when depressed, grounds diode X2 (Fig. 6-15) through a contact-multiplying diode because lead "B" (Fig. 6-17) is thereby grounded. This enables the long-sustain function. The carillon stop tab also disables the tibia tremulant/vibrato and turns off four tibia keyers:

      3rd—Third (Chime "E")
      8ve—Octave (4' Piccolo)
      12th—Twelfth (2⅔' Twelfth)
      15th—Two Octaves (2' Piccolo)

Typical trouble symptoms are as follows:

Diode X2 shorted or leaky (Fig. 6-15): The note associated with the diode will cipher when the long-sustain function is not turned on.

Diode X2 open (Fig. 6-15): The note will have no sustain characteristic because the sustain capacitor cannot charge.

Diode X3 leaky or shorted (Fig. 6-15): The note will have undesired sustain characteristics.

Diode X3 open (Fig. 6-15): The note has no sus-tain characteristic because the charged capacitor cannot discharge through the oscillator.

Contact-multiplying diode open (Fig. 6-17): The associated keyer cannot be turned on by the harp or carillon stop tab.

Contact-multiplying diode shorted (Fig. 6-17): The stops associated with that sustain stop (harp or carillon) will also be turned on whenever the stop associated with the shorted diode is turned on.

Example: If the carillon stop contact-multiplying diode for the 2⅔' twelfth becomes shorted, the 2⅔' twelfth stop tab will turn on the entire carillon.

TREMULANT/VIBRATO VOICING CIRCUITS AND TROUBLES

In the example under discussion, two tremulant functions are provided: The Unit Tibia Tremulant/Vibrato (turned on by the Tibia Tremulant and Tibia Vibrato stop tabs), and the Main Tremulant/Vibrato (turned on by the Main Tremulant and Main Vibrato stop tabs). As shown in Fig. 6-18, the tremulant/vibrato generator is a form of RC oscil-lator that develops a 7-Hz sine-wave output. A po-tentiometer is provided to adjust the oscillating fre-

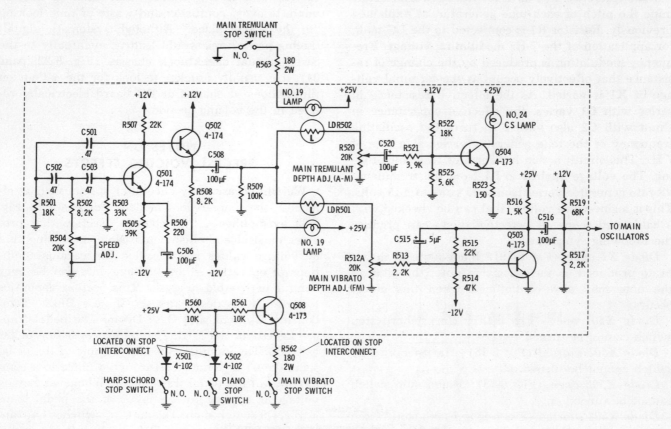

Fig. 6-18. Typical tremulant/vibrato generator.

quency; a second potentiometer controls the percentage of amplitude modulation; a third potentiometer controls the deviation of the frequency modulation. In this example, the tremulant generator runs continuously. The tremulant stop tab turns on a light-dependent resistor (LDR) when a-m output is desired, and the vibrato stop tab turns on another LDR when fm output is desired.

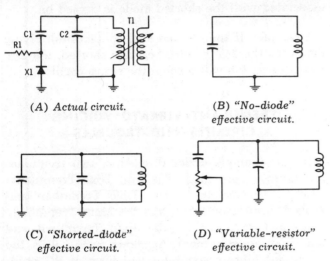

(A) *Actual circuit.*

(B) *"No-diode" effective circuit.*

(C) *"Shorted-diode" effective circuit.*

(D) *"Variable-resistor" effective circuit.*

Fig. 6-19. Frequency modulation of a tone generator.

With reference to Fig. 6-19, LC networks determine the pitch of each tone generator, as explained previously. Resistor R1 is connected to the LC tank, for application of the 7-Hz modulating voltage. Frequency modulation is produced by the change of resistance that effectively occurs as the terminal voltage of X1 is varied. As the effective resistance in series with C1 varies, the effective capacitance in shunt with C2 also varies. In turn, the oscillating frequency of the tone generator varies at a rate of 7 Hz. This circuit action is a form of resistance tuning. The voltage applied to R1 from the tremulant/vibrato generator varies from −15 volts to +15 volts. This is a sine-wave voltage that can be checked with a calibrated scope. A defective diode can produce the following symptoms:

Diode X1 open (Fig. 6-19): Inadequate or no vibrato produced on the associated note; the pitch of the note may also be detuned when this defect occurs.

Diode X501 open (Fig. 6-18): Harpsichord stop switch cannot be turned on.

Diode X501 shorted (Fig. 6-18): Harpsichord stop switch cannot be turned off.

Diode X502 open (Fig. 6-18): Piano stop switch cannot be turned on.

Diode X502 shorted (Fig. 6-18): Piano stop switch cannot be turned off.

LOCALIZATION OF DEFECTIVE COMPONENTS

Localization of defective components in the voicing section often involves both electrical and mechanical considerations. For example, with reference to Fig. 6-20, the flute voice will be "dead" in case C607 shorts, because the audio signal is conducted directly to ground as a result. Of course, other defects could also "kill" the flute voice; to confirm the suspicion, we will make a resistance measurement across C607. If the ohmmeter reads zero, or nearly so, the suspicion is thereby confirmed. On the other hand, a resistance reading of approximately 12 kilohms clears C607 from suspicion. But before the test can be made, we must locate the capacitor in the chassis or on a PC board. Let us consider this procedure.

From the schematic of the voicing section (Fig. 6-20), we would tend to believe that C607 would be found on the voicing section circuit board. Therefore, we turn to the associated PC board layouts diagrammed in Fig. 6-21. However, check of the callouts fails to reveal C607. Although most of the voicing-section components are located on a PC board in this example, a few are mounted on a separate chassis. This is a possibility that must be kept in mind, to avoid confusion and waste of time looking "in the wrong place." Although systematic signal-tracing procedures would lead us eventually to the Swell-manual cheekblock chassis (Fig. 6-22, page 84), it is usually quicker to look for the callout on illustrations of chassis or PC board electrically related to the voicing section.

NOTES ON SPECIAL VOICING EFFECTS

We will occasionally encounter special voicing effects in the more recent models. For example, Fig. 6-23 exemplifies a "toy-counter" section that provides musical embellishments. Note in passing that dc voltage values are specified for various conditions of operation—these voltage data can be very helpful in trouble analysis. This section generates tones for stops designated as Chinese Block, Tambourine, Cymbal, and Bass Drum. The pedal traps are keyed via the keying amplifier consisting of Q9 and Q10. The keying point of each note of the pedal signal keyer is connected through a diode to a common bus of the pedal traps keyer. Whenever keying voltage is applied to the input of the pedal traps keyer, Q9 switches on. This in turn switches on transistor Q10. The output of Q10 is +12 volts dc, and is

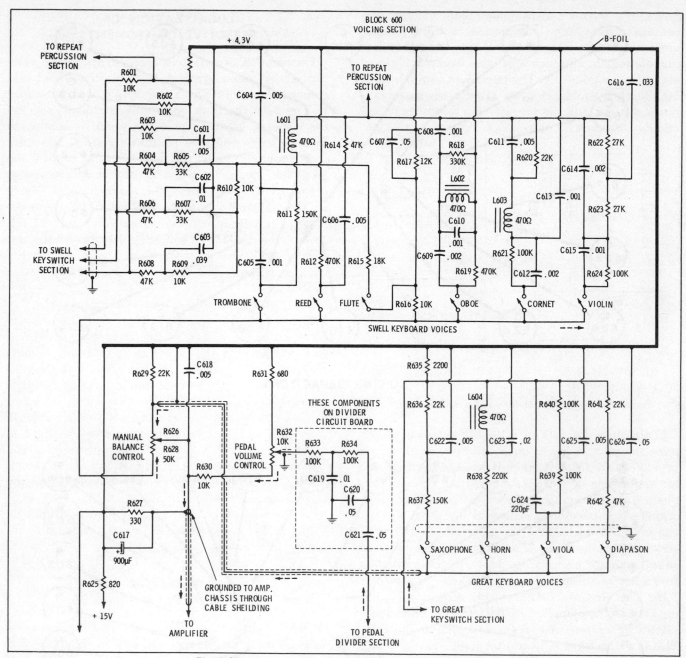

Fig. 6-20. Voicing section for a home-entertainment organ.

applied as keying voltage to the bass-drum and the cymbal subsections.

The bass-drum waveform is produced in Fig. 6-23 by an RC oscillator that has insufficient gain to sustain oscillation. When a pedal key is depressed, a trigger pulse is applied to the quiescent oscillator through R110, C112, and X8. Note that when the bass-drum stop switch is open, X8 is reverse-biased so that the trigger pulse will not be applied to the quiescent oscillator. On the other hand, when the bass-drum stop tab is depressed, the stop switch is closed, which removes the reverse bias from X8 and

permits the trigger pulse to be applied to the quiescent oscillator. This trigger pulse shock-excites the bass-drum oscillator circuit; it suddenly comes out of quiescence and proceeds through a transient ringing period.

This ringing waveform is a damped sine wave, as typified in Fig. 6-24. The length of time that the circuit rings is determined by the setting of the Stability potentiometer R92, in Fig. 6-23. Improper adjustment of this potentiometer can cause a cw output, due to self-oscillation. Note that the Pitch control, R88, determines the ringing frequency. Since

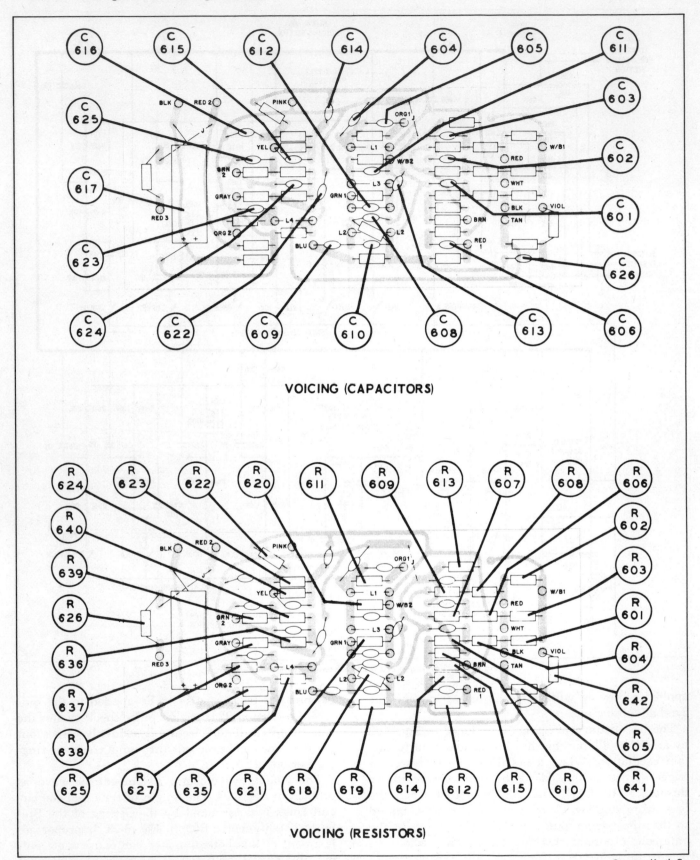

VOICING (CAPACITORS)

VOICING (RESISTORS)

Courtesy Heath Co.

Fig. 6-21. Voicing-section components.

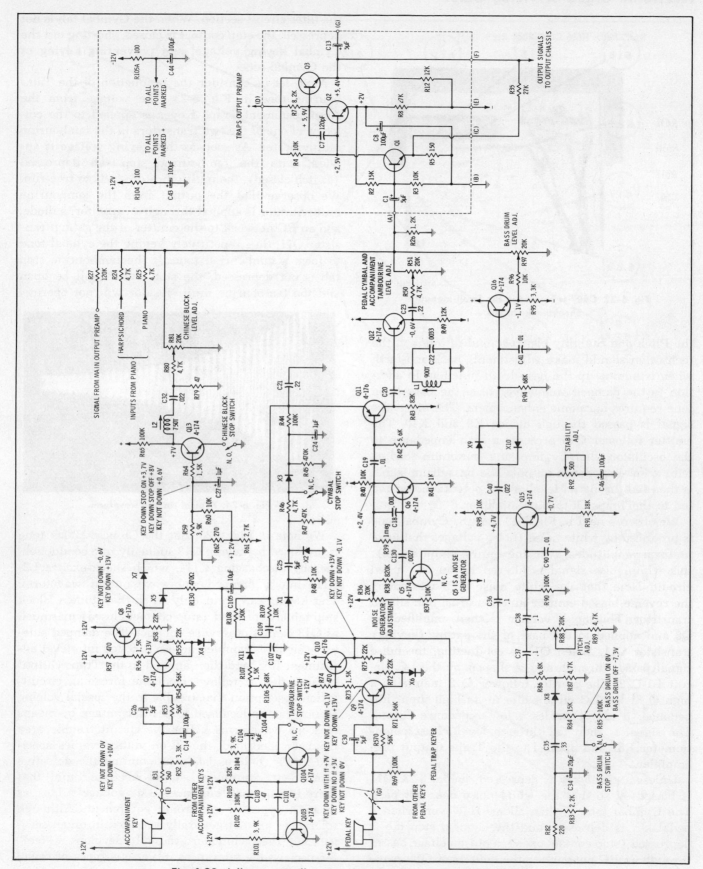

Fig. 6-23. A "toy-counter" section that provides special voicing effects.

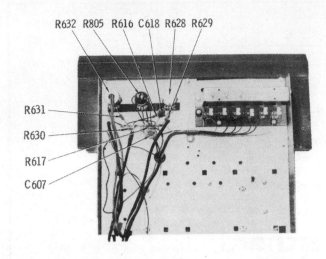

R632 R805 R616 C618 R628 R629

R631

R630

R617

C607

Courtesy Heath Co.

Fig. 6-22. C607 is located in the Swell-manual cheekblock chassis.

the Pitch and Stability controls tend to interact, the technician should make adjustments back-and-forth when trimming up the bass-drum function. In addition to the damped sine-wave basis, the bass-drum tone requires harmonic enhancement. Therefore, the signal is passed through diodes X9 and X10. The emitter follower Q16 presents a high impedance to the oscillator, thereby imposing minimum loading with a low-impedance output. The bass-drum signal is then fed through a level-adjust potentiometer and fed to the Traps Output preamplifier.

We observe next in Fig. 6-23 that the Cymbal tone is produced by white noise (noise voltages that have uniform amplitudes over the entire audio range); this white-noise signal is filtered by an LC tuned circuit. Note that the white noise is generated by the reverse-biased emitter junction of an npn silicon transistor. This noise voltage is then amplified by Q6 and applied to the base of the gating (keying) transistor Q11. When Q11 is conducting, the noise signal passes through and is shaped by the LC circuit L1-C22. The emitter follower Q12 maintains a high Q in the LC circuit due to its high input impedance; it also provides a low-impedance output. The signal is then fed through level-adjust potentiometer R51 and applied to the Traps Output preamplifier.

Unless a pedal key is depressed in Fig. 6-23, Q11 is biased off so that the white noise does not pass. The Cymbal tone is then silent. However, when a pedal key is depressed and the Cymbal stop tab is depressed (stop contact open), a pulse voltage passes through an RC network to the emitter of Q11, causing it to conduct; thus, the white noise is passed to

the filter circuit section. When the Cymbal tab is not depressed, the stop contact is closed, shorting out the Cymbal keying voltage, and preventing keying of the Cymbal tone.

Next, let us consider the production of the Tambourine tone in Fig. 6-23. The voltage from the Accompaniment Traps Keyer is applied to the collector of one of the two transistors in the tambourine multivibrator. As soon as this keying voltage is applied, with the tambourine stop tab depressed (switch closed), the multivibrator starts to free-run. We observe that the output from the tambourine multivibrator is applied through a capacitor, a diode, and an RC network to the emitter of the gating transistor Q11, thus repetitively keying the cymbal tone to form a tambourine tone. If the tambourine stop tab is not depressed, the stop switch will be open and the tambourine multivibrator will not operate.

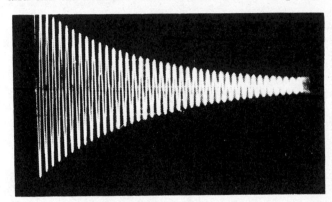

Fig. 6-24. Typical ringing waveform.

We note in Fig. 6-23 that the Chinese Block tone is produced by keying Q13 suddenly into conduction, thereby discharging C114, which shock-excites L2-C114 into a damped sine-wave output waveform. This keying can occur only when the Chinese Block stop tab is depressed (stop contact closed) inasmuch as Q13 cannot otherwise conduct. The damped sine-wave signal is sampled across R66, fed into level adjustment R68, and then applied to the Traps Output preamplifier. It follows from the foregoing circuit-action description that trouble in the special voicing section can be localized to best advantage by means of scope waveforms. After the circuit trouble area has been identified, the off-on voltage values specified in Fig. 6-23 assist in pinpointing the defective component. Beginners should keep in mind that there is a normal tolerance on dc voltage values, as in most types of electronic equipment. Although tolerances are not generally specified in organ service data, the technician gradually develops a "feel" for permissible tolerances in various types of organ circuitry.

Chapter 7

Piano/Harpsichord, Glockenspiel, and Special Voicing Networks

Piano tones are sometimes classified as percussive tones; both piano and harpsichord voices are described as chromatic percussive tones. On the other hand, nonchromatic percussive tones are exemplified by drum, cymbal, wire-brush, bell, and woodblock tones. That is, chromatic percussive tones are characterized by a dominant pitch. All percussive tones have a comparatively fast attack; a piano waveform rises rapidly to a brief peak, followed by a rapid decay interval, and terminates in a slow decay at low amplitude. Fig. 7-1 shows the wave envelope of a piano tone. When a section of the waveform is greatly expanded, its detail appears as shown in Fig. 7-2. A harpsichord tone has a similar waveform, with the exception that its attack is faster and its peak is sharper. Glockenspiel tones (also called orchestra bells) are mechanically generated. They are customarily generated by striking metal bars with magnetically actuated hammers. Fig. 7-3 shows

the bars in an optional glockenspiel unit. Bell tones are richer in harmonics than piano tones, and the fourth harmonic will often be the dominant pitch. One category of bell tones has no dominant pitch, and is accordingly included in the class of nonchromatic percussive tones.

GENERAL DISCUSSION

Although piano and harpsichord voicing networks are generally built into the more elaborate electronic organs, various members of the more specialized voices such as glockenspiel tones are often optional, and are provided as an accessory. A spare tab stop may be provided to accommodate an optional

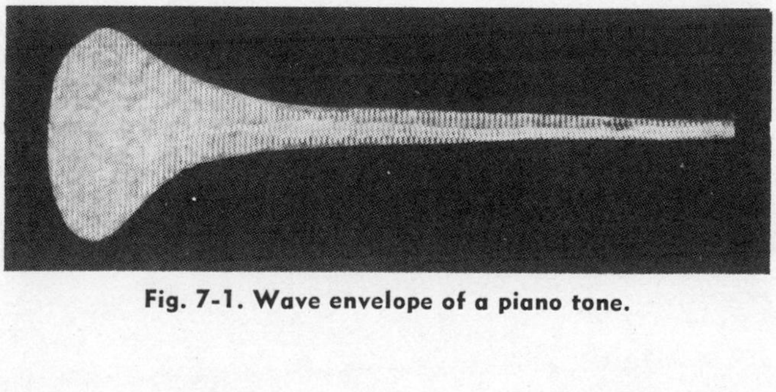

Fig. 7-1. Wave envelope of a piano tone.

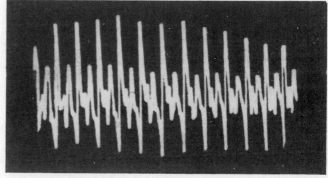

Fig. 7-2. Expanded section of a piano-tone waveform.

Fig. 7-3. View of tone bars in a glockenspiel unit.

voice, and the assembly may either be fabricated in an individual case, or designed for installation inside the organ console. In the former case, exterior cabling is required from the console. As would be anticipated, the circuit actions employed for generation of percussive tones are basically different from those used to generate diapason tones. Therefore, it is helpful to analyze typical networks in some detail.

PIANO/HARPSICHORD VOICING NETWORKS

A typical piano/harpsichord voicing network is driven by half-rectified sine waves. To obtain the required percussive effect, a special keying network is used. Separate voicing networks are employed for piano and harpsichord tones. In the example of Fig. 7-4, the piano-signal keyer operates from a sine-wave source. When a manual key is depressed, this sine-wave signal is rectified and fed to a preamplifier. A more detailed diagram is shown in Fig. 7-5. Note that the signal keyer diode X4 will not conduct un-

less its anode is more positive than its cathode. Since the sine-wave voltage passes through both positive and negative values, it would pass through X4 on each positive half cycle if it were not for the positive bias voltage that is applied to X4 via R11 from R102 and R103. Thus, X4 is cut off unless a manual key is depressed, whereupon X4 has a net bias of zero and the positive half cycles of the sine-wave signal pass into the piano preamplifier.

The percussive characteristic is introduced by means of the special keying network seen in Figs. 7-4 and 7-5. Depressing a manual key applies a positive voltage to the voltage divider R110 and R6. In turn, a positive voltage is applied to capacitor C6. A resistive ground return is provided by R7 and X2. Thus, C6 charges through R7. At the instant of contact, there is a +6-volt drop across R7. In turn, C8 is charged with great rapidity via R8 and X3. Diode X4 therefore conducts, and operates as a half-wave rectifier. Next, as C6 continues to charge, less voltage drops across R7, so that diode X4 conducts less of the sine-wave signal. Finally, X4 is once more completely cut off.

We observe that the bias network of R98 and R99 in Figs. 7-4 and 7-5 allows the capacitor to charge very rapidly until the drop across R7 falls below the bias-network voltage. At this time, the capacitor can charge only through R7 at a much slower rate. This circuit causes the keying voltage on the signal diode to rise rapidly to maximum when the key is first depressed and to fall rapidly while C6 goes through its first charging mode, but to fall slowly when C6 goes through its second charging mode. If the key should

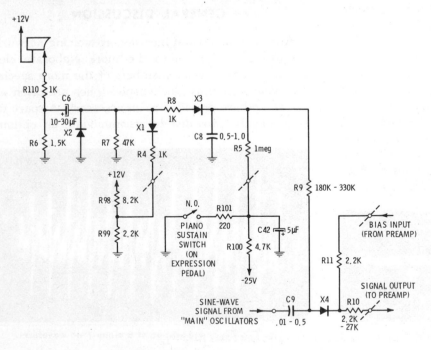

Fig. 7-4. Circuit of a piano-voice keyer.

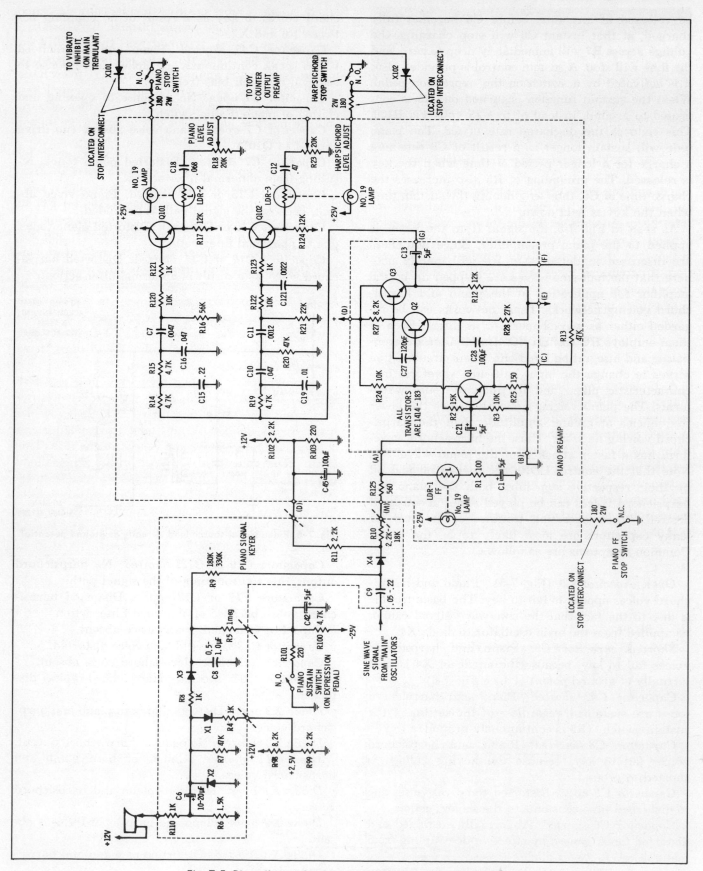

Fig. 7-5. Piano/harpsichord voicing networks and keyer circuitry.

be released at any time before C6 becomes fully charged, at that instant C6 will stop charging, the voltage across R7 will immediately drop to zero, and the tone will stop. A sustain control is provided also; it is activated by a switch on the expression pedal. When the sustain function is turned on, R5 is connected to ground, instead of to −25 volts via R100. This reduces the discharge rate of C8. The piano tone will sustain longer as a result of C8 retaining a charge for a longer period of time when the key is released. The grounding of R5 also increases the charge time of C6, thus lengthening the sustain time when the key is held down.

As seen in Fig. 7-5, the signal from the keyer is applied to the piano preamplifier. Since amplifiers are discussed in detail later, we will merely note here that the half-sine waves are stepped up by the amplifier for application to the piano and harpsichord voicing networks. These networks can be regarded either as waveshapers, or as filters. Each of them employs RC circuitry in combination differentiating and integrating functions. Their circuit action serves to change the input half-sine waveform into characteristic piano and harpsichord tonal waveforms. The piano voicing network passes the lower frequencies at greater amplitude than the harpsichord voicing network. Thus, the harpsichord waveform has a faster attack than the piano waveform. Note that the control LDRs are turned on and off by their respective stop tabs; both the piano and harpsichord voices can be played simultaneously, if desired. When operating troubles occur, open or leaky capacitors are most likely to be the cause. Common symptoms are as follows:

Open capacitor C9 (Fig. 7-5): Piano and harpsichord voices appear to fail to key. The basic trouble is due to the fact that the sine-wave signal cannot be applied from the main oscillator to diode X4.

Shorted capacitor C9: Piano and harpsichord voices fail to key, because the anode of X4 is held virtually at ground potential (see Fig. 7-6).

Capacitor C42 shorted: Piano and harpsichord tones are sustained, regardless of the setting of the sustain switch. (R5 is continuously grounded.)

Capacitor C8 shorted: Piano and harpsichord voices fail to key, because the keying voltage is shorted to ground.

Capacitor C8 open: Distorted tonal response, due to disturbed time constants in the keyer section.

Capacitor C6 shorted: Abnormally sustained and distorted tones, caused by effective dc coupling from manual key to keyer diode.

Capacitor C6 open: Failure of piano and harpsi-

chord voices to key as a result of no coupling between R6 and X2.

Capacitor C45 shorted: Piano and harpsichord voices speak continuously, or cipher, in response to removal of cutoff bias from X4.

Capacitor C1 open: No response to opening and closing of piano ff stop switch.

Capacitor C7 open: Piano voice absent (no drive applied to Q101).

Capacitor C7 shorted: Distorted piano tones, resulting from abnormal filter action.

Capacitors C15 or C16 shorted: Piano voice absent, because the signal path is grounded.

Capacitors C15 or C16 open: Distorted piano tones, due to abnormal filter action.

Capacitors C10 or C11 shorted: Distorted harpsichord voice, as a result of abnormal filter action.

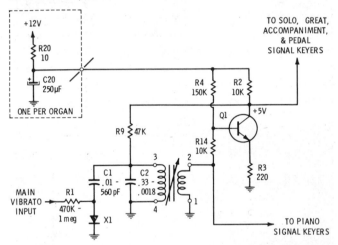

Fig. 7-6. Piano signal-source lead virtually at ground potential.

Capacitors C19 or C121 shorted: No harpsichord output, due to grounding of the signal path.

Capacitors C19 or C121 open: Distorted harpsichord voice, because of abnormal filter action.

Capacitor C18 open: Piano voice absent.

Capacitor C18 shorted: Piano voice distorted.

Capacitor C12 open: Harpsichord voice absent.

Capacitor C12 shorted: Harpsichord voice distorted.

Diode X2 open: Distortion of both piano and harpsichord voices.

Diode X2 shorted: No piano or harpsichord output.

Diode X1 shorted: Cipher of both piano and harpsichord voices.

Diode X1 open: Distorted piano and harpsichord voices.

Diode X3 open: Piano and harpsichord voices absent.

Diode X3 shorted: Distortion of piano and harpsichord voices.

Diode X4 shorted: Ciphering of piano and harpsichord voices.

Diode X4 open: Piano and harpsichord voices apparently fail to key.

GLOCKENSPIEL ARRANGEMENT AND OPERATION

A glockenspiel unit may be provided with an individual cabinet, as illustrated in Fig. 7-3. It may alternatively be designed as a subpanel that mounts under the lid of the organ console, as shown in Fig. 7-7. The glockenspiel voice is radiated directly from the metal bars; that is, the tone is not processed through the amplifier and tone cabinet. This arrangement provides maximum tonal realism. With reference to Fig. 7-8, an electromechanical striker assembly is employed, with a solenoid actuator. Each solenoid is driven by a transistor; since the striker must be retracted quickly to avoid muffling the tonal waveform, the transistor is keyed through a differentiating circuit. This differentiating circuit ensures that the solenoid will be energized uniformly, regardless of time that the key may be depressed.

Fig. 7-7. Glockenspiel unit fabricated as a subpanel.

Since a solenoid is an inductor, the counter-emf that is generated when Q1 stops conducting must be bypassed and dissipated. Otherwise, the collector junction of the transistor is likely to be damaged. This is the function of diode X1. Therefore, if transistor Q1 burns out and must be replaced, check X1 also. Troubleshooting of this category of electromechanical circuitry is facilitated by specification of the key dc operating voltages. The scope is of little assistance, because only dc switching circuits are involved. Since the emitter and base of Q1 are normally at the same potential, the transistor is cut off. However, when a key is depressed, a positive transient voltage is applied; most of this keying volt-

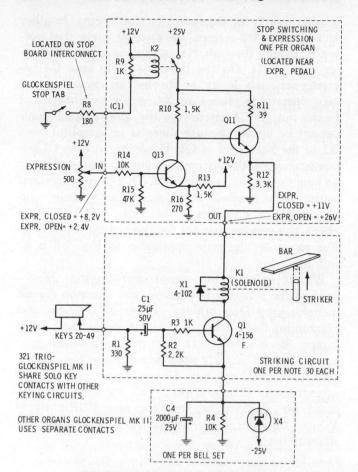

Fig. 7-8. A glockenspiel configuration.

age is applied to the base, which causes the transistor to conduct.

Note in Fig. 7-8 that the collector supply circuit is open when the glockenspiel stop tab is open. When the tab is closed, relay K2 pulls on, and the collector supply line is then connected to Q1. Transistors Q11 and Q13 operate in the collector supply line to control the exact collector voltage applied to Q1. That is, when the expression control is varied through its range, the dc collector voltage applied to Q1 also varies from 11 volts to 26 volts. Therefore, more current flows through the striker solenoid when the expression control is operated at maximum volume. Since more current flows through the solenoid, the striker is moved faster and there is more sound output from the metal bar. If the striker operates erratically, it is advisable to check out the mechanism first. For example, if lint or dust collects between the striker and its concentric tube, friction may weaken or stop the normal travel of the striker. An air blast application usually suffices to clean the mechanism.

When trouble occurs in the circuitry of the unit, defective capacitors are ready suspects. With reference to Fig. 7-8, if C4 opens up, the striker operates weakly due to the degeneration that occurs. In other words, when C4 is open, the current surge that normally passes through K1 is attenuated by the resistance of R4. On the other hand, in case C4 becomes seriously leaky, or shorted, an excessive current demand is placed on X4, which overheats and burns out. If C1 opens up, the glockenspiel voice cannot be keyed because there is no coupling from R1 to the base lead of Q1. However, in case C1 becomes shorted, the striker remains up against the bar as long as the key is depressed. This causes the tonal output to be muffled. When making dc voltage measurements in a system of this type, it is helpful to check the service manual for the wiring color code. For example, the code applicable to Fig. 7-8 is as follows:

White: ground for signal and keying. *Black:* ground for relays, LDR lamps, and common for all switching by stop tablets, crescendo, presets, and sforzando. *Red:* +15 volts dc for relays and LDR lamps. *Black-White:* −12 volts dc regulated for preamps. *Red-White:* +12 volts dc regulated for keying, tremulants, and preamps. *Green-White:* −25 volts dc unregulated. *Brown-White:* +25 volts dc unregulated for glockenspiel, presets, and LDRs. *Blue-White:* 20 volts ac for music rack and stopboard illumination.

REPEAT-PERCUSSION FUNCTION

As its name indicates, a repeat-percussion tone is basically a percussion waveform that is automatically repeated at a predetermined rate. Fig. 7-9 illustrates a typical repeat-percussion waveform. With reference to Fig. 7-10, a typical repeat-percussion network is shunted across the voicing circuits. When the ON-OFF switch is open, the complex signal in the voicing section is unaffected. However, when the switch is closed, the complex signal is interrupted at a rate determined by the repeat-percussion control setting (R805). The circuit operation is as follows:

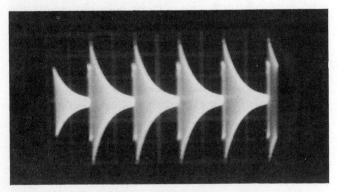

Fig. 7-9. Repeat-percussion waveform.

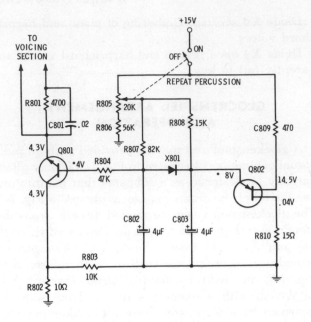

Fig. 7-10. Repeat-percussion circuit.

When the repeat-percussion switch is turned on, a +15 volt dc potential is applied to R805 and R806. Capacitor C803 begins to charge through R808. At the same time, C802 charges through R807, but at a slower rate. This slower charging action maintains diode X801 in a nonconducting condition. When the charge on C802 rises above +4.3 volts, transistor Q801 is forward-biased through R804. In turn, Q801 conducts and shunts the complex voice signal to ground, thus interrupting the signal. Next, when C803 charges above the firing level of unijunction transistor Q802, C802 and C803 discharge through the base and thence to ground. Note that the frequency of switching is determined by the rapidity of attaining firing voltage for Q802. This circuit action is as follows:

When the repeat-percussion control R805 (Fig. 7-10) is turned counterclockwise, the voltage applied to R808 decreases. This causes C803 to take longer to charge to the firing voltage of Q802, resulting in slower switching. On the other hand, when the repeat-percussion control is turned clockwise, the voltage applied to R808 is increased. In turn, C803 takes less time to charge to the firing voltage of Q802, resulting in faster switching action. When C802 suddenly discharges via Q802, Q801 is abruptly cut off. Therefore, the complex voice signal rises at once to its peak amplitude. As in most circuitry of this variety, defective capacitors are the most probable troublemakers.

With reference to Fig. 7-10, note that if C802 opens up, Q801 conducts continuously. In turn, the organ voices fail to speak as long as the repeat-percussion

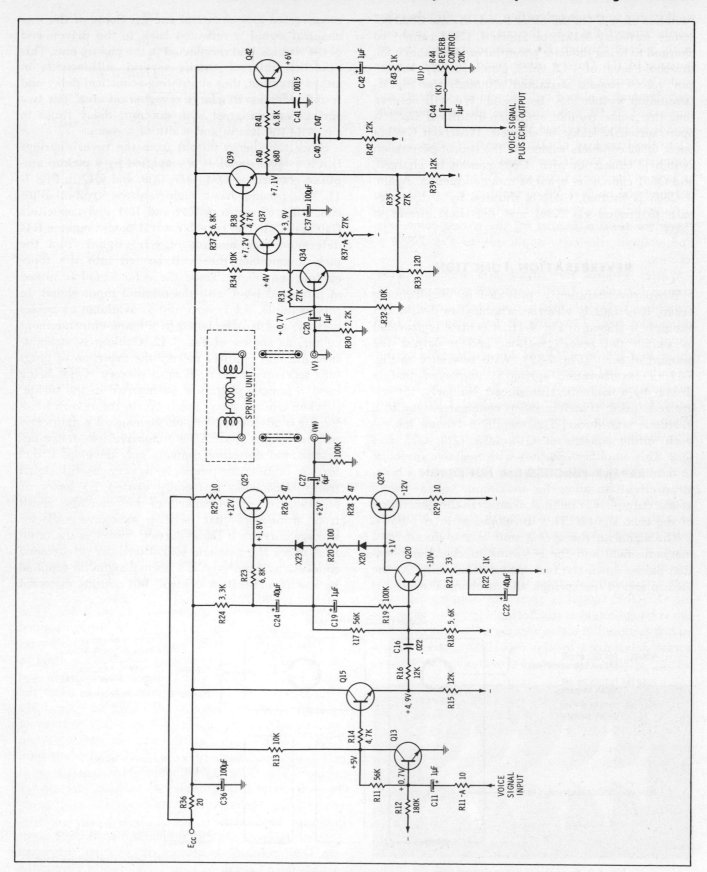

Fig. 7-11. An electromechanical reverberation unit.

switch is closed. On the other hand, in case C802 becomes seriously leaky, or shorted, C802 cannot be charged to bring the base potential of Q801 above the threshold level of +4.3 volts. Consequently, the organ voices remain sustained although the repeat-percussion switch may be closed. We will observe that this same trouble symptom results if C803 is open, seriously leaky, or shorted. That is, if C803 is open, Q802 conducts whenever the repeat-percussion switch is closed. In turn, C802 cannot be charged, and Q801 cannot be brought into conduction. Again, if C803 is shorted, C802 is shunted by a discharge path to ground via X801 and the short circuit in C803.

REVERBERATION FUNCTION

When reverberation is provided by an electronic organ, it is usually electromechanical in design. An example is shown in Fig. 7-11. A control is provided to switch the reverb section, and to adjust the amount of echo (Fig. 7-12). With reference to Fig. 7-11, a reverberation spring is employed that is driven by a magnetic transducer; similarly, the energized spring transfers its mechanical energy to a magnetic transducer. The amplifier driving the reverb spring consists of Q13, Q15, Q20, Q25, and Q29. This amplifier operates with negative feedback to minimize distortion. C24 and R24 provide a bootstrap circuit to allow for maximum voltage swing at the output. It is helpful to analyze the generation of the echo signals. This development is as follows.

The signal in the spring unit is introduced by a magnetic field and the resulting mechanical vibration passes down the two spring delay lines. At the pickup end of the springs, the mechanical energy is reconverted into electrical energy. Some of the mechanical signal is reflected back to the driven end of the springs, and rereflected to the pickup end. This reflection interval entails several milliseconds in either direction, thus simulating acoustical delay and sound reflection in a large reverberant area. The two springs are designed with different delay times to simulate the length and width of a room.

Since the energy output from the reverb springs is a low-level signal, it is amplified by a pickup amplifier comprising Q34, Q37, Q39, and Q42 in Fig. 7-11. This preamp has a high-frequency roll-off filter consisting of resistors R40 and R41 and capacitors C40 and C41. The reverb control potentiometer R44 determines the amount of echo signal from the pickup amplifier that will be fed into the tone-cabinet amplifiers. Thus, the echo signal is mixed at a desired level with the original input signal. In this example, the reverb unit is available as an accessory, and it is included in a home-entertainment center, as shown in Fig. 7-12. Cabling is straightforward, and requires merely the insertion of plugs into accessory sockets. If an accessory is not being used, a jumper plug must be inserted in the socket.

When trouble symptoms occur in the reverb function, it is advisable to check the control potentiometer and switch first. After extensive use, noisy operation and defective contacts may develop. If distortion occurs, the scope is a very useful signal tracer. Distortion is usually caused by leaky or otherwise defective capacitors, but can also result from transistors that develop excessive collector leakage current. If the distortion occurs in the input lead, check the plug and socket for poor or corroded connections. Similarly, if a normal signal is supplied by the reverberation control, but sounds distorted

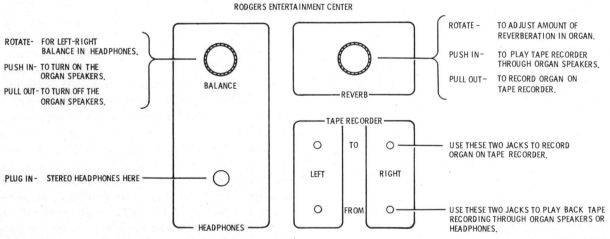

Courtesy Rodgers Organ Co.

Fig. 7-12. Reverberation control unit with switching and attenuation functions.

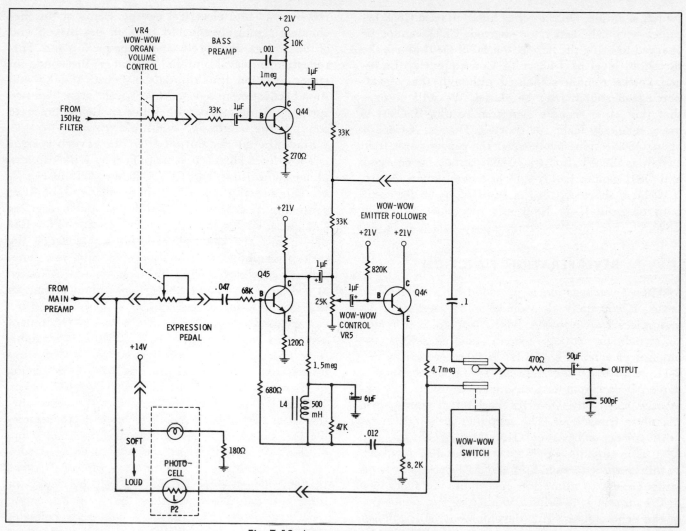

Fig. 7-13. A wow-wow voicing section.

or weak when reproduced from the tone cabinet, check the output plug and socket for poor or corroded connections.

WOW-WOW FUNCTION

Some electronic organs provide a slow vibrato effect, called wow-wow, that can be used with various voices. This is a descriptive term that tends to indicate the sound effect that is produced. The action is automatic when the wow-wow switch (located on the expression pedal) is closed. Fig. 7-13 shows a wow-wow voicing section, with the switch in its closed position. The input voice signal is taken from the preamp outputs at the junction of the 33k-ohm resistors. We observe that the wow-wow preamp and emitter follower will operate as a low-frequency oscillator when the wow-wow switch is closed. In turn, a slow vibrato is impressed on the voice signal that is being processed.

As explained previously, trouble symptoms in this type of circuitry are usually tracked down to defective capacitors. Note that if the lamp bulb in the photocell unit burns out, the wow-wow function will be barely audible, or absent, due to the high effective series resistance in the feedback loop. LDRs are normally very long-lived, but may deteriorate occasionally. A substitution test is advisable. Resistors are also very stable units in low-voltage circuits, but will gradually drift in value with the passage of years. Cumulative tolerances may eventually result in failure of an oscillator to operate normally. Inductors seldom cause trouble unless mechanically damaged or corroded due to an unfavorable atmospheric environment. In case a transistor develops a short circuit and must be replaced, an abnormal current drain may be set up that overheats one or more of the associated resistors. In this situation, a substantial increase in resistance value may result.

Chapter 8

Amplifier Servicing

Power requirements for amplifiers used in electronic organs were noted previously. A small organ may contain only one amplifier, whereas a large organ designed for concert-hall installation may operate with several amplifiers, as exemplified in Fig. 8-1. It has also been noted that large tone cabinets may be fabricated with individual amplifiers. Although an organ amplifier may have high-fidelity characteristics, this is not necessarily the case. That is, an organ is designed to produce certain musical tones, whereas a hi-fi amplifier is designed to reproduce musical tones. The present trend is to solid-state amplifiers with output-transformerless (OTL) design. However, large numbers of vacuum-tube amplifiers are still in use, and require periodic servicing.

GENERAL DISCUSSION

It is helpful to start analysis of amplifier troubles with vacuum-tube configurations. Fig. 8-2 exemplifies the simplest form of RC-coupled triode amplifier. The most common source of trouble (apart from defective tubes) is leakage in the coupling capacitor, which upsets the grid bias of the tube. Cathode bias is commonly used, and pentode tubes are often used instead of triodes, because of their comparatively high gain. For example, Fig. 8-3 shows a pentode input-amplifier configuration. This type of circuitry uses more capacitors, and hence is more likely to develop trouble symptoms because of capacitor defects. For example, if C4 opens up, V1 operates in a degenerative mode, and the stage gain is impaired. Or, if C4 shorts, the grid/cathode bias is disturbed and the stage distorts. In case C5 opens up, there will be audio signals on the grid of V1. Furthermore, the stage gain is reduced and the frequency response of the circuitry is altered. Similar symptoms occur if C5 short circuits.

Trouble in a given circuit is sometimes caused by a defect in the preceding circuit. For example, in Fig. 8-4, a short circuit or heavy leakage condition in C_c will cause seriously abnormal screen and plate current in V2. It is quite likely that the plate-load, screen-dropping, and cathode-bias resistors for V2 will be badly overheated or burned out during the process of destruction of V2. Similarly, this type of trouble can change the value of a circuit resistor, even if it is not burned out. In such a case, the amplifier starts working again when C_c is replaced, but normal operation is not resumed. Let us briefly consider the factors that are involved:

1. When a cathode resistor is much too high in value, the grid/cathode bias is excessive. Stage gain is reduced, and distortion will occur on high-level signals if a sharp-cutoff pentode is used.
2. When a plate-load resistor is much too high in value, the stage gain is increased to some extent; however, the dynamic range of the stage is reduced, and overload distortion occurs on high-level signals. High-frequency response is also impaired.
3. When a screen-dropping resistor is much too high in value, the stage gain is reduced and overload distortion occurs on high-level signals.

Transformer coupling is widely employed in the output stage of a vacuum-tube amplifier, as seen in

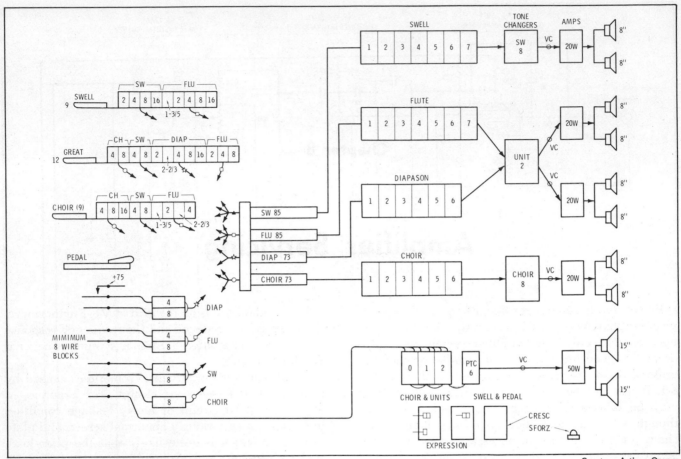

Fig. 8-1. Block diagram of a concert organ.

Courtesy Artisan Organs

Fig. 8-3. A simple transformer-coupled interstage configuration is shown in Fig. 8-5. Except in special-purpose vacuum-tube amplifiers, transformer interstage coupling is avoided, simply because high-performance audio transformers are comparatively costly devices. In either output or interstage transformers, common causes of trouble symptoms are as follows:

1. Primary winding of transformer burned out, due to preceding circuit fault that imposes an excessive current demand.
2. Leakage to core or between windings caused by absorption of moisture or by serious overheating.
3. Response will sometimes be impaired if the primary or secondary leads are reversed accidentally. (In negative-feedback systems, uncontrollable oscillation nearly always results.) Negative feedback is explained below.
4. Distortion due to shorted cathode-bypass capacitor.
5. Low gain due to open bypass capacitor.

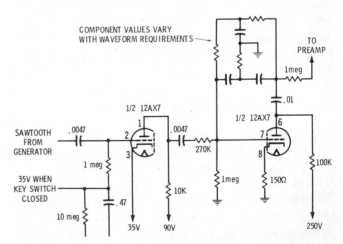

Fig. 8-2. Typical circuit used in a percussion preamplifier.

NEGATIVE FEEDBACK

When a portion of the audio output voltage is fed back to the input of the same or a preceding stage in opposite phase to the applied signal, negative feedback is present and degeneration takes place. A circuit that provides degeneration is called an inverse

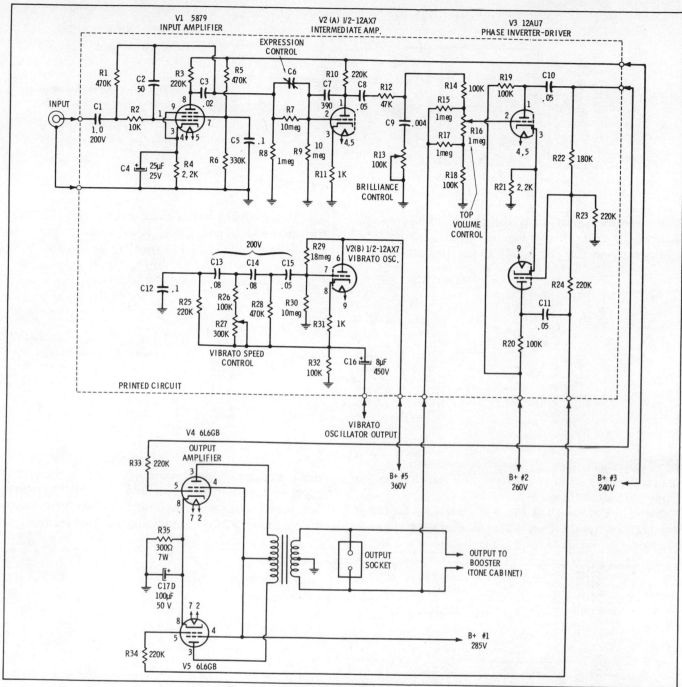

Fig. 8-3. Amplifier with pentode input stage.

or negative-feedback circuit. When degeneration is present, the voltage fed back opposes the applied input voltage and therefore reduces its amplitude, as exemplified in Fig. 8-6. Since the feedback voltage subtracts from the applied input signal, the stage gain is reduced. However, the disadvantage of reduced gain is offset by a reduction of frequency and amplitude distortion. The stability of the circuit is also improved. In repairing a negative-feedback loop, it is important to use replacement parts with com-

paratively close tolerances, to restore normal operation.

The two basic types of feedback configurations are called *constant-voltage feedback* and *constant-current feedback*. Two basic circuit arrangements are shown in Fig. 8-7. In Fig. 8-7A, the voltage divider consisting of R1 and R2 is connected across the plate circuit of an audio-output tube. Capacitor C between the two resistors prevents the dc plate voltage from being applied to the grid of the tube. The voltage di-

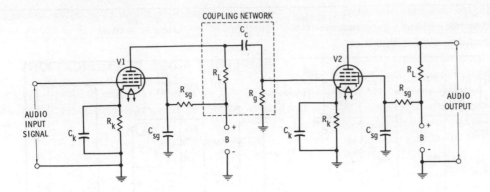

Fig. 8-4. Typical RC-coupled amplifier using pentodes.

vider applies a portion of the audio-output voltage back to the grid. This voltage is equal approximately to the fraction $R2/(R1 + R2)$ times the output volt-

age. This feedback voltage is in series with the input transformer secondary and is in opposite phase to the voltage induced in that winding by the preceding

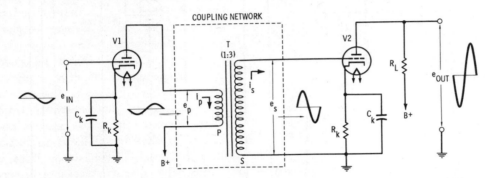

Fig. 8-5. Transformer-coupled amplifier using triodes.

amplifier stage. We call this circuit action constant-voltage feedback, since its magnitude depends on the audio-output voltage.

Next, in the circuit of Fig. 8-7B, negative feedback is obtained by omitting the bypass capacitor across

the cathode-bias resistor. The portion of the output signal voltage dropped across R opposes the signal input voltage between grid and ground. Therefore, degeneration takes place, and the stage gain is reduced. This method of applying negative feedback is

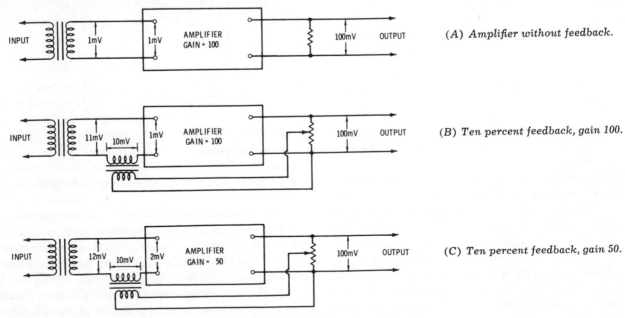

(A) *Amplifier without feedback.*

(B) *Ten percent feedback, gain 100.*

(C) *Ten percent feedback, gain 50.*

Fig. 8-6. Effects of degenerative feedback.

called constant-current feedback, because the feedback voltage is proportional to the cathode current. We will find that much more elaborate feedback circuits are often used in deluxe electronic organs. However, the basic principle remains the same. When negative feedback is carried around two or more stages, it becomes increasingly important to maintain exact replacement-component values—particularly of capacitors, which affect signal phase

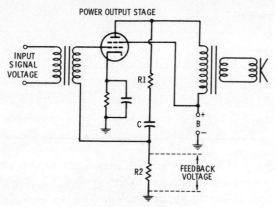

(A) *Voltage-divider feedback.*

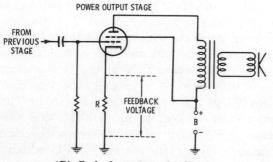

(B) *Cathode-resistor feedback.*

Fig. 8-7. Negative-feedback circuits.

shift. For example, if a leaky capacitor in an elaborate negative-feedback circuit is replaced by a wide-tolerance unit, uncontrollable oscillation might develop at very low or very high audio frequencies.

Systematic troubleshooting in vacuum-tube amplifier circuitry can be summarized as follows:

1. Check tubes first, or try substituting new tubes.
2. If there is no audio output, use a scope to trace the signal through the amplifier.
3. After a defective stage is localized, measure dc voltages and compare the measured values with those specified in the organ service data.
4. In case of doubt, disconnect one end of a suspected capacitor and test it with a capacitor checker, or make a substitution test.
5. Make supplementary resistance measurements of controls, fixed resistors, and transformer

windings to confirm these as possible sources of trouble.

AMPLIFIER MODE CLASSIFICATIONS

It is helpful to briefly note the various classes of operation employed by organ amplifiers. They are:

1. Class-A operation.
2. Class-B operation.
3. Class-AB operation.
4. Class-AB_1 operation.
5. Class-AB_2 operation.

In Class-A operation, the tube is normally biased so that there is space current from cathode to plate at all times. The operating point is determined by the grid bias, and is usually chosen midway between cutoff and plate-current saturation. The output plate waveform is practically undistorted in normal operation. However, overdrive will cause peak compression or clipping. In Class-B operation, the tube is normally biased at or near plate-current cutoff. Thus, there is plate current during the positive half cycle of the grid input signal, but there is no output during the negative half cycle of grid drive. Thus, in a single-ended stage, the output waveform is seriously distorted. This mode of operation is used in waveshapers. If a Class-B amplifier is designed to amplify with negligible distortion, a stage includes two tubes operating in push-pull. Note that there may be grid current at maximum drive.

An intermediate mode of amplifier action is called Class-AB operation. This type of amplifier employs a tube that is biased in the region between Class-A and Class-B. There is plate current for more than one-half, but for less than the entire, cycle in normal operation. Two subclasses are also defined for this mode of operation. A subscript 1 (Class-AB_1) denotes that there is no grid current at maximum rated power output. Again a subscript 2 (Class-AB_2) denotes that there is grid current when the stage is driven to maximum rated power output. As in the case of a Class-B stage, two tubes are provided in a Class-AB stage when the output waveform must be practically undistorted. The advantages of a Class-AB amplifier are its greater power output, compared with a Class-A amplifier, and its lower distortion, compared with a Class-B amplifier. A summary of amplifier characteristics is given in Table 8-1.

It should not be supposed that Class-A operation is entirely free from distortion. A triode provides less distortion than a pentode, and a high value of

Table 8-1. Amplifier Characteristics

Class	Location of Operating Point on Dynamic Characteristic	Relative Distortion	Relative Power Output	Approximate Percentage of Plate Efficiency
A single-tube	On linear portion	Low	Low	Under 20%
A push-pull		Very low	Moderate	20 to 30%
AB single-tube	Between linear portion and plate-current cutoff	Moderate	Moderate	40%
AB push-pull		Low	High	50 to 55%
B single-tube	At vicinity of cutoff	High	High	40 to 60%
B push-pull		Low	Very high	60 to 65%

plate-load resistance minimizes residual distortion. However, a triode is not an entirely linear device, and there is appreciable distortion present at moderate power output, with maximum tolerable distortion at maximum rated power output. Therefore, a push-pull Class-A amplifier is employed when a tone must be amplified with minimum distortion. The remaining distortion can be decreased by means of negative feedback, but this also involves a "trade-off" in the form of increased driving-signal requirements. Some organs include hi-fi stereo reproduction facilities in a section called an entertainment center; this is an example of an application for amplifier facilities with distortion reduced to a practical minimum.

DIRECT-COUPLED AMPLIFIERS

We will find direct-coupled stages in some of the older-model organs; as explained subsequently, direct coupling is widely used in late-model solid-state organ amplifiers. A basic example of a direct-coupled amplifier using triodes is shown in Fig. 8-8. The advantage of this design is that it can amplify very low bass signals with minimum distortion by means of very simple circuitry. A voltage divider is generally used to supply the necessary dc operating voltages for the amplifier from a regulated power supply. The B+ supply voltage is applied across the voltage-divider resistor R_d, which is tapped at suitable points. Capacitor C_d is used to bypass any ac voltage variations that might appear across R_d. The audio-output voltage is amplified by V1 and V2, and appears as the audio-output voltage at the plate of V2 in normal operation. The plate-load resistor R_{L1} also serves

as the grid resistor for V2, inasmuch as the voltage drop across it is applied to the grid of V2. R_{L2} serves as a plate-load resistor for V2.

Note that the cathode of V1 is connected to point A, and that the plate is connected to point B on the voltage divider in Fig. 8-8. Point B is positive with respect to point A, which makes the plate positive with respect to the cathode. This voltage relationship permits V1 to conduct. Note that the voltage developed from point A to ground serves as bias voltage for V1. It is necessary for the plate of V2 to be positive with respect to its cathode, and the grid voltage of V2 must not be positive with respect to its cathode. The plate current of V1, which flows through R_{L1}, produces a considerable voltage drop

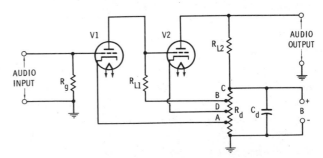

Fig. 8-8. Typical direct-coupled amplifier using triodes.

across this resistor. In turn, the voltage at the plate of V1 and at the grid of V2 is less positive than at point B on the voltage divider. Tap D is located at a point on resistor R_d such that the magnitude of the positive voltage on the grid of V2 is lower than that of the positive voltage on the cathode of V2. Therefore, the grid of V2 is actually less positive (or is effectively negative) with respect to the cathode of

V2 in normal operation. The voltage between points C and D is the plate voltage for V2.

When trouble symptoms are encountered in direct-coupled stages of a vacuum-tube amplifier, the most likely causes are as follows:

1. A tube may have developed grid current because of grid emission or traces of gas. A substitution test is preferred.
2. Regulation of the power supply may be unsatisfactory; a common cause is aging of a voltage-regulator tube.
3. The bypass capacitor for the voltage divider may be leaky or open.
4. A fixed resistor (particularly of the composition type) will occasionally develop thermal instability.
5. Corroded contacts or imperfect connections are especially troublesome in direct-coupled stages.

PHASE INVERSION

Many organ amplifiers have phase-inverter stages, as exemplified in Fig. 8-3. Since distortion is small at low signal levels, but increases rapidly at high levels in Class-A amplifier, it is desirable to change from single-ended input to double-ended output. Thus, the phase inverter V3 in Fig. 8-3 is driven from the single-ended output of R16, and processes this signal into a double-ended drive signal for the output amplifier V4 and V5. This phase-inverter stage employs a twin triode in a paraphase configuration. The cathodes of the triodes are biased by a common cathode resistor, R21. Since R21 is unbypassed, the signal voltage drops across the resistor; in turn, the cathode of the lower tube is driven by the cathode of the upper tube. However, the upper tube is grid-driven, whereby the triode plate outputs are 180° out of phase with each other. Thus, V4 and V5 are driven in push-pull.

Single-tube phase inverters are also found in various organ-amplifier systems. For example, the second half of the 12AU7 in Fig. 8-9 operates in this manner. The plate-load resistor has a value of 22k ohms, and the unbypassed portion of the cathode resistor also has that value. In turn, each of these resistors develops an output signal; the output signals have equal amplitudes, but are 180 degrees out of phase with each other. Accordingly, the 6L6 tubes are driven in push-pull. Trouble symptoms in phase-inverter stages are caused by the same types of defects as are encountered in single-ended configurations. That is, leaky or open capacitors are the most probable troublemakers. However, in a phase-in-

verter configuration, resistor values are somewhat more critical, inasmuch as a push-pull amplifier has minimum distortion only when both tubes are equally driven. To check for output balance in a phase inverter, apply a scope in turn at the two outputs, to see whether the waveform amplitudes are equal. If the amplitudes are unequal, look for an off-value load resistor.

SOLID-STATE INVERTERS AND AMPLIFIERS

Since transistors are fabricated in both pnp and npn configurations, we encounter a number of novel circuits in solid-state amplifiers, compared with vacuum-tube amplifiers. When the transistors in a circuit are all of the same type, such as pnp, the basic circuitry is analogous to vacuum-tube designs. However, there is nevertheless an important distinction, in that any transistor is basically a current-operated device, rather than a voltage-operated device. With reference to Fig. 8-10, a split-load phase inverter is shown, with Q1 driving a push-pull output amplifier stage comprising Q2 and Q3. The path of output current from Q1 is through R3 and also through R2. Note that R2 and R3 normally have equal values, and the base-bias voltage is determined by the value of R1. The signal analysis is as follows:

When the input signal aids the forward bias in Fig. 8-10 (driving the base more negative), the output current I_o increases. This increased output current causes the top terminal of R3 to become more positive with respect to ground, and the top terminal of R2 becomes more negative with respect to ground. On the other hand, when the input signal opposes the forward bias, the foregoing changes are reversed. Thus, a pair of output signals are produced that are 180° out of phase with each other. In turn, Q2 and Q3 are driven in push-pull.

Since the arrangement in Fig. 8-10 tends to distort on high-amplitude input signals, due to the inequality of emitter and collector internal impedances, electronic organs often use the arrangement shown in Fig. 8-11. R4 compensates for the foregoing inequality, and the proportions of R2 and R3 are chosen to provide a balanced drive to Q2 and Q3. The gain of a one-stage phase inverter is quite low, and comparatively high-level drive is required. Additional gain will be provided by a phase-inverter stage if it employs two transistors, as exemplified in Figs. 8-12 and 8-13. The arrangement in Fig. 8-12 is called a common-emitter/common-base inverter, and the configuration in Fig. 8-13 is called a common-emitter/common-emitter inverter. As in the case of

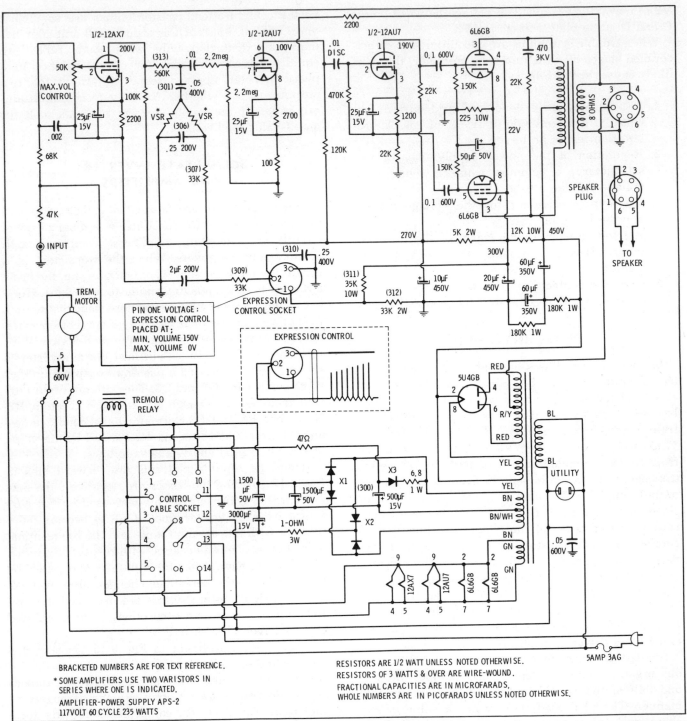

Fig. 8-9. Amplifier with a single-tube phase inverter.

tube-type inverters, a scope is very useful to check whether the two outputs have equal amplitudes.

Solid-state power (or output) amplifiers are almost always operated in push-pull. In the example of Fig. 8-14, a transformer is used for phase inversion and to match the output impedance of Q3 to the input impedances of Q4 and Q5. The preamplifier employs direct-coupled stages; this section is analogous to the vacuum-tube counterpart exemplified in Fig. 8-8. Although preamplifier stages are necessarily operated in Class A, the output stage is usually operated in Class AB or Class B. Fig. 8-15 shows a simplified circuit for a Class-B push-pull zero-bias amplifier. Each transistor normally conducts on alternate half cycles of the signal. In turn, the half cycles are combined in the secondary of the output transformer. Theoretically, distortionless amplification would be obtained. In practice, however, commercial transistors have appreciable nonlinearity in the vicinity of collector-current cutoff. This leads to a form of distortion called crossover distortion. It can be minimized by operating the transistors in Class AB. For example, the output transistors in Fig. 8-14 are forward-biased by 0.2 volt, and operate

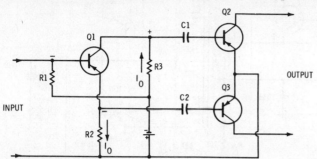

Fig. 8-10. Basic circuit for a one-stage phase inverter.

in Class AB. This is termed biasing to *projected cutoff;* this mode of operation is not always included in the Class-AB category, since only a slight quiescent current is permitted.

Fig. 8-16 shows the essentials of a Class-B amplifier biased to projected cutoff. Note that a bypass capacitor *must not* be connected across R1. Otherwise, the base-bias voltage increases as the input signal amplitude increases, and serious distortion

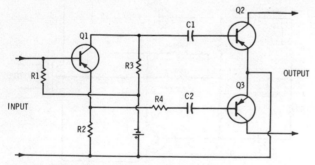

Fig. 8-11. One-stage phase inverter that includes equalized output impedance.

can occur. In other words, the base-emitter junction of a transistor operated in Class-B has rectifier action, and will develop self-bias if the common-emitter resistor is shunted with a bypass capacitor. This self-bias voltage, if appreciable, can result in clipping the signal waveform. The same general principle applies to RC coupling in a Class-B amplifier (Fig. 8-17). With reference to Fig. 8-17A, when Q1 is driven into conduction, it leaves a positive charge on the right-hand plate of C1 after the half cycle has passed. Therefore, Q1 is now reverse-biased. The charge on C1 cannot escape through Q1, because the

reverse resistance of the base-emitter junction is very high. The charge on C1 can flow only through R3, which must have an undesirably low resistance value to avoid distortion. That is, the stage gain is low; the low-frequency response is also impaired.

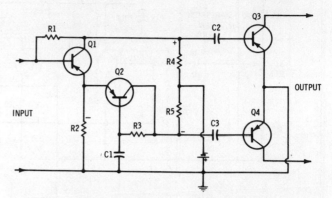

Fig. 8-12. Two-stage phase inverter using two transistors in a common-emitter and a common-base configuration.

To obtain good frequency response, high gain, and low distortion, diodes are used instead of resistors in the base-return circuit, as shown in Fig. 8-17B. When Q1 is driven into conduction, electrons flow from the right-hand plate of C1 into the base. However, the positive charge on C1 is not trapped in this case, because as the half cycle of drive decreases in amplitude, electrons flow through X1 in sufficient numbers to prevent build-up of signal-developed bias. Good frequency response is obtained in normal operation, because a diode normally has very high back resistance. Therefore, when Q1 is being driven into conduction, X1 is out of the circuit from a practical point of view. Since audio signal does not flow through X1, the stage develops high gain. Maintenance of projected-cutoff bias at all times ensures that negligible distortion will occur.

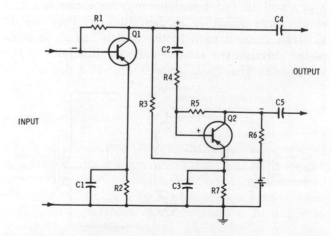

Fig. 8-13. Two-stage phase inverter using two transistors in the common-emitter configuration.

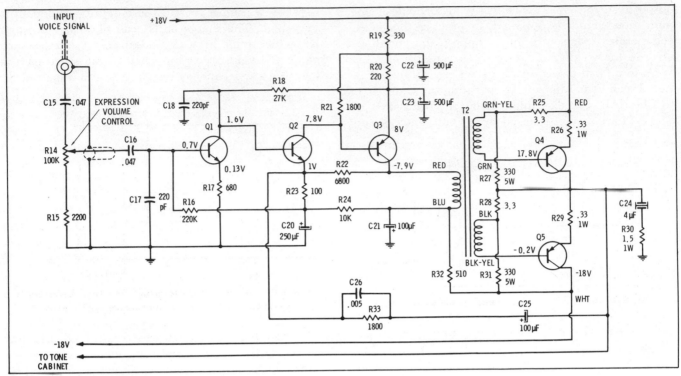

Fig. 8-14. Typical organ amplifier.

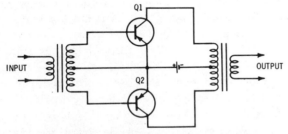

Fig. 8-15. Basic circuit for Class-B, push-pull amplifier with zero base-emitter bias.

Complementary-symmetry amplifiers are also employed in modern organ design. Fig. 8-18 shows how a pnp and an npn transistor may be connected in a single-stage amplifier configuration so that the dc electron current path in the output circuit is completed through the emitter-collector junctions of the transistors. This basic arrangement is called a com-

plementary-symmetry circuit. It has the advantage of dispensing with a phase-inverter driver stage, and does not require a center-tapped transformer. Note

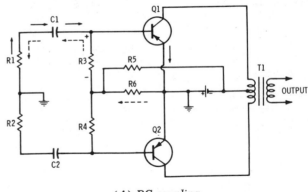

(A) RC coupling.

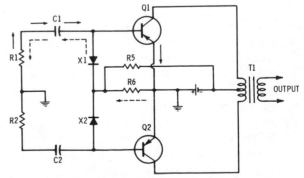

(B) Capacitance-diode coupling.

Fig. 8-17. Class-B, push-pull configurations.

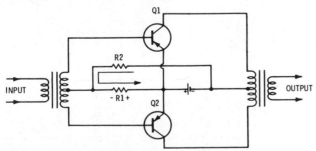

Fig. 8-16. Class-B, push-pull amplifier circuit using a small forward bias.

that this configuration also eliminates the need for discharge diodes, which are required for efficient operation when capacitance coupling is used in ordinary configurations. The complementary-symmetry output circuit employs a parallel connection to load R1, and thereby eliminates the need for a tapped-primary transformer in the output circuit. As in any push-pull stage, replacement transistors should be reasonably well matched to avoid distortion. In normal operation, there is no dc current through the load R1, which is a useful fact in troubleshooting procedures. That is, if a dc voltmeter connected across R1 gives an appreciable reading, we know that there is a fault in the circuit operation.

In other complementary-symmetry configurations, a small forward bias is applied to the base-emitter junctions of the transistors, as shown in Fig. 8-19.

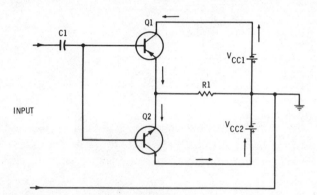

Fig. 8-18. Basic zero-bias complementary-symmetry circuit.

Bias currents are bled from the collectors to the bases by resistors R2 and R3, which form a voltage divider in combination with R1. Normally, the value of R1 is very small, so that it has a negligible unbalancing action on the audio signal. This arrangement has the advantage of minimizing residual crossover distortion. As in the case of the zero-bias arrangement, there is normally no direct current through R_L. Therefore, the output from the ampli-

fier can be applied directly to the voice coil of a speaker, thus dispensing with an output transformer. If a dc voltmeter indicates a voltage drop across the voice coil, we know that there is a fault in the circuit operation.

Elaborate amplifiers sometimes employ audio-output sections with direct-coupled complementary-symmetry stages, as shown in Fig. 8-20. In Fig. 8-20A, a common-emitter complementary-symmetry stage comprising Q3 and Q4 is directly driven by the preceding complementary-symmetry stage comprising Q1 and Q2. Single-ended drive is applied to Q1 and Q2. This arrangement provides high gain, good frequency response, and eliminates the need for a phase inverter and an output transformer. In Fig. 8-20B, the configuration provides high input resistance. The signal voltage dropped across R_L develops negative feedback in the input circuit of Q1 and Q2, thereby developing a high input resistance. Negative feedback also improves the linearity of amplifier action at high output levels. As in the previous example, there is normally no dc voltage drop across R_L, which makes this a key check point in case malfunction is suspected. Dc voltage measurements are generally the most useful approach to pinpointing a defective component in the amplifier system.

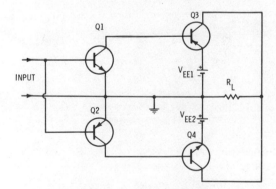

(A) *Normal input resistance.*

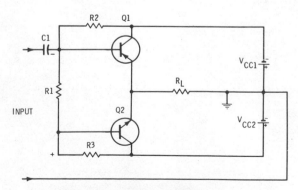

Fig. 8-19. Complementary-symmetry circuit with small forward bias.

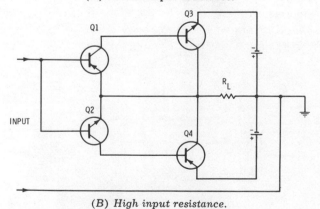

(B) *High input resistance.*

Fig. 8-20. Examples of direct-coupled complementary-symmetry stages.

Chapter 9

Troubleshooting Power Supplies

Most organ power supplies employ comparatively involved circuitry. Even in the smaller instruments, power supplies are more elaborate than those usually found in other home-entertainment equipment. Nearly all organ power supplies provide both positive and negative outputs, which are often closely regulated. Larger instruments contain power supplies that meet heavy current demands. It is perhaps an unexpected aspect of design that the earlier organs required the most demanding power-supply units. A typical modern power supply that exploits the possibilities of solid-state devices is shown in Fig. 9-1. This configuration provides positive and negative dc outputs, two of which are closely regulated. An ac output is also provided. Each output branch includes a circuit breaker to avoid component damage in case of accidental overload.

GENERAL DISCUSSION

The basic half-wave rectifier arrangement is shown in Fig. 9-2. A semiconductor rectifier may be used instead of a vacuum diode. Since the rectifier is energized from a 60-Hz source, the fundamental ripple frequency is also 60 Hz. The ripple is reduced by capacitive filtering in the first analysis. For example, Fig. 9-3 shows the basic capacitance filter. A capacitor is connected across the load. In turn, the dc-voltage component is increased and the ripple is reduced. Filter action also changes the half-sine ripple waveform into a semisawtooth ripple waveform. Note that if the load resistance had an infinite resistance value, the ripple amplitude would be zero.

On the other hand, as the load approaches a short circuit, the ripple amplitude increases and approaches the half-sine waveform as a limit.

Fig. 9-4 illustrates basic full-wave rectifier operation. Since both halves of the source ac waveform are rectified, the fundamental frequency is 120 Hz. A capacitor connected across the load provides the basic filter configuration. In turn, the dc-voltage component is increased and the ripple is reduced. If the load resistance has an infinite value, the ripple amplitude is zero. On the other hand, as the load approaches a short circuit, the ripple amplitude increases and approaches the full-rectified sine waveform as a limit. Note that the foregoing examples of basic power supplies provide positive dc output only. Organ power supplies generally provide both positive and negative dc outputs. The fundamental circuitry that is employed can be explained by means of the oppositely polarized rectifiers shown in Fig. 9-5. Each rectifier operates in a half-wave circuit with individual filter capacitors. Note that if the output is taken from the positive and negative lines, and the ground is not used, double output voltage becomes available.

Positive and negative dc outputs can also be provided by full-wave rectifier circuits, as exemplified in Fig. 9-6. Full-wave rectification provides an advantage in that it is easier to filter. The modern trend is to simplify filter circuitry by utilizing very large filter capacitors. For example, the configuration in Fig. 9-6 employs 2000-μF filter capacitors. This simplification became possible only with the development of unusually high capacitance values. For

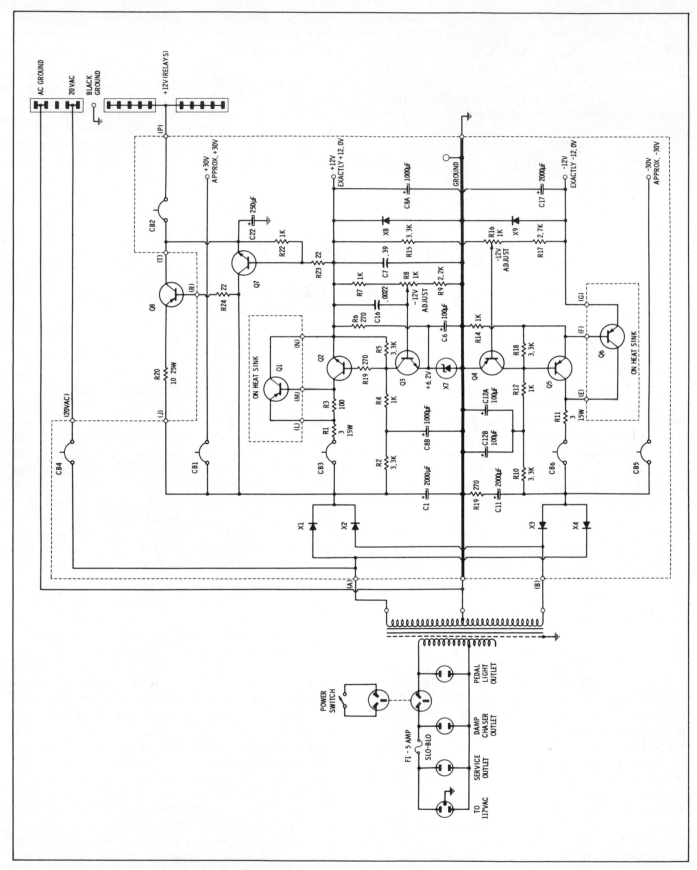

Fig. 9-1. Typical power supply for a modern organ.

example, we will find power supplies in older-model organs (Fig. 9-7) with filter capacitors ranging in value from 5 to 50 μF. In turn, multiple-pi section RC filter networks were used to reduce the ripple voltage satisfactorily. A disadvantage of an RC filter circuit is its comparatively poor regulation; that is, the output voltage decreases as the current demand increases.

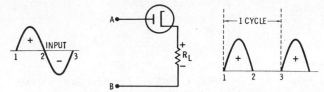

Fig. 9-2. Basic half-wave rectifier operation.

Regulation can be improved by using one or more LC sections in a power supply, as exemplified in Fig. 9-8. That is, an inductor has comparatively low dc resistance, but has a high ac reactance. However, inductors are expensive and heavy, which militates against their use in power-supply design. The arrangement in Fig. 9-8 is called a choke-input filter; although its output voltage is somewhat less than that of a capacitor-input filter (Fig. 9-7), the choke-input filter provides better regulation. In other words, the output voltage does not fall as fast when the current demand is increased, as shown in Fig. 9-9. However, tone generators usually require practically constant supply voltage, regardless of line-voltage fluctuations. To meet this requirement, some

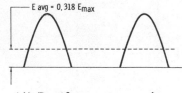

(A) Rectifier output waveform.

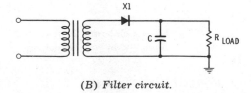

(B) Filter circuit.

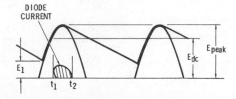

(C) Load-voltage and diode-current waveforms.

Fig. 9-3. Basic capacitance filter.

form of electronic voltage regulation is employed. For example, note the voltage regulator tubes V7 and V8 in Fig. 9-8.

ELECTRONIC VOLTAGE REGULATION

The simplest type of voltage regulator is a glow tube connected in series with a current-limiting resistor, as shown in Fig. 9-10A. Good regulation is provided, although the current capability of a glow

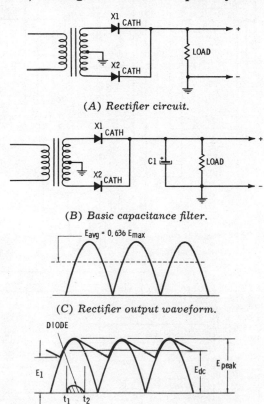

(A) Rectifier circuit.

(B) Basic capacitance filter.

(C) Rectifier output waveform.

(D) Load-voltage and diode-current waveform.

Fig. 9-4. Basic full-wave rectifier operation.

tube is somewhat limited. The glow tube also provides filtering, and reduces ripple to a very low level. However, it is desirable to use a reasonable amount of filtering prior to the glow tube, because a high-level input ripple reduces the output-current capability of the tube. Note that the value of R cannot be made less than a value determined by the maximum current rating of the glow tube. That is,

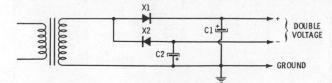

Fig. 9-5. Power supply arrangement for positive and negative outputs.

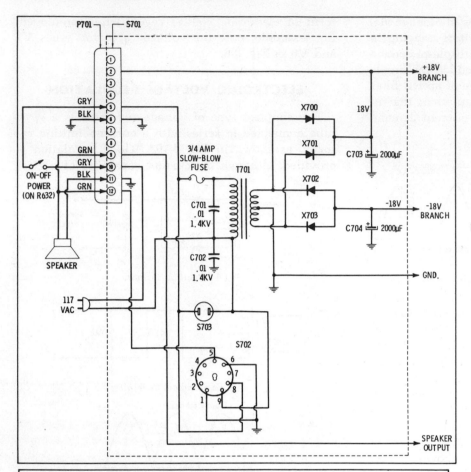

Fig. 9-6. Full-wave rectification with positive and negative dc outputs.

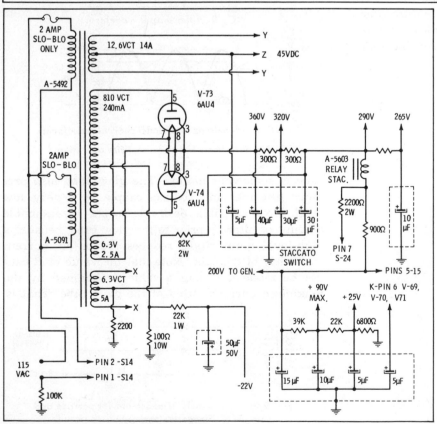

Fig. 9-7. An elaborate filter configuration found in an early model organ.

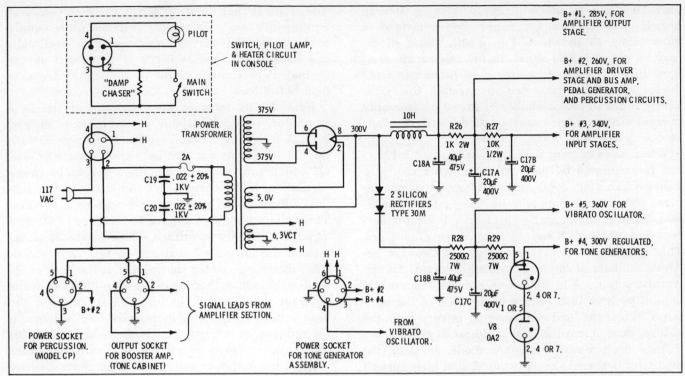

B+ #1, 285V, FOR AMPLIFIER OUTPUT STAGE.

B+ #2, 260V, FOR AMPLIFIER DRIVER STAGE AND BUS AMP, PEDAL GENERATOR, AND PERCUSSION CIRCUITS.

B+ #3, 340V, FOR AMPLIFIER INPUT STAGES.

B+ #5, 360V FOR VIBRATO OSCILLATOR.

B+ #4, 300V REGULATED, FOR TONE GENERATORS.

Fig. 9-8. Organ power supply with an LC filter section.

when the load current demand is absent, the glow tube is required to pass all of the current flowing through R.

Glow tubes are rated at various voltage drops, for example, 105 volts. When comparatively high voltage is to be regulated, two or more glow tubes can be connected in series, as exemplified in Fig. 9-

10B. However, only the output-voltage capability is increased; the output-current capability remains the same as for one tube. If desired, the permissible output current may be divided among two or more

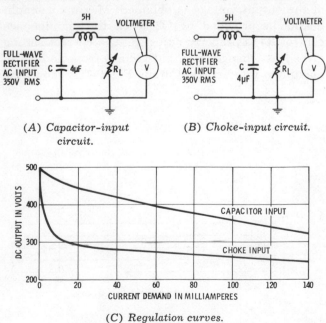

(A) Capacitor-input circuit.

(B) Choke-input circuit.

(C) Regulation curves.

Fig. 9-9. Comparison of capacitor-input and choke-input filters.

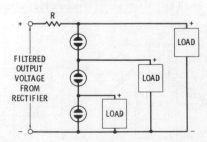

(A) Single glow-tube circuit.

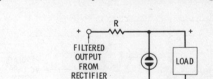

(B) Glow tubes in series for higher voltage output.

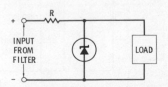

(C) Zener-diode voltage regulator.

Fig. 9-10. Simple voltage-regulator circuits.

loads that require different supply voltages. Modern organs generally employ zener diodes instead of glow tubes, as shown in Fig. 9-10C. Zener diodes may be connected in series, in the same manner as glow tubes. Note that neither glow tubes nor zener diodes should be connected in parallel; this error would result in the possibility of throwing the entire current burden on one tube, or diode, with resulting device destruction.

When more current is demanded by the load than can be regulated by glow tubes or zener diodes, a voltage-regulator configuration employing one or more power transistors is used. The basic circuit arrangement is shown in Fig. 9-11. In this circuit, current flows through R and the zener diode at all times. This produces a constant-voltage bias source between the base of the transistor and ground. An npn transistor is used in this example; the zener diode applies positive bias voltage to the base of the transistor. When the load resistance R_L is very high, the voltage drop across the load is almost as great as the voltage drop across the zener diode. In turn, the transistor is biased almost to cutoff, and little current is supplied to the high-resistance load. On the other hand, when the load resistance R_L is low, the voltage drop across the load starts as a much smaller value than the voltage drop across the zener diode. But now, the transistor is forward-biased, and the transistor supplies much more current to the load.

The result is that the drop across the load comes to equilibrium at a value almost (but not quite equal) to the high-resistance load condition. The small voltage variation that does occur is expressed as the regulation percentage of the power supply from no load to full load.

Next, let us consider the operation of the two-transistor voltage-regulator circuit shown in Fig. 9-12. A full-wave bridge rectifier is employed, with Q1 functioning as a controlled variable resistor, and Q2 functioning as a dc amplifier to obtain closer regulation. If the current demand changes, the output voltage of the power supply will tend to vary. This voltage change is applied to the base of Q1 as a dc negative-feedback voltage, which increases or decreases the effective resistance of Q1. Let us consider the case in which the voltage at the base of Q2 tends to decrease, thereby causing an increase in the collector voltage, and, in turn, an increase of the base voltage on Q1. This increase of base voltage on Q1 reduces its internal resistance, which increases the output voltage across the load. On the other hand, if the output voltage tends to increase, the circuit action will increase the internal resistance of Q1, and thereby decrease the output voltage across the load.

Note that the function of the zener diode in Fig. 9-12 is to provide a fixed dc voltage reference; the temperature coefficient of the zener diode also helps to compensate for output voltage changes due to the temperature coefficient of transistor Q1. By providing dc amplification through Q2, closer regulation of the output voltage is obtained. Maximum amplification is provided by Q2 when the maintenance control R4 is properly adjusted. The correct setting gives least change in output voltage from no load to maximum rated current drain. Fig. 9-12B shows the

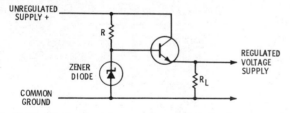

Fig. 9-11. The basic elements of a regulated voltage supply.

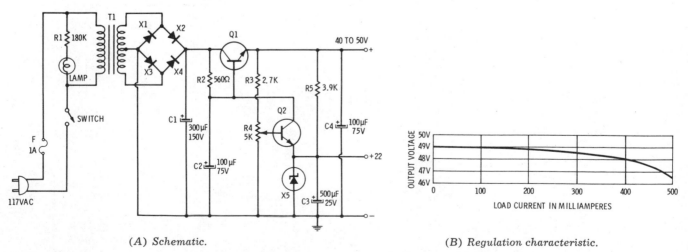

(A) Schematic.   (B) Regulation characteristic.

Fig. 9-12. Voltage regulation using transistors and a zener diode.

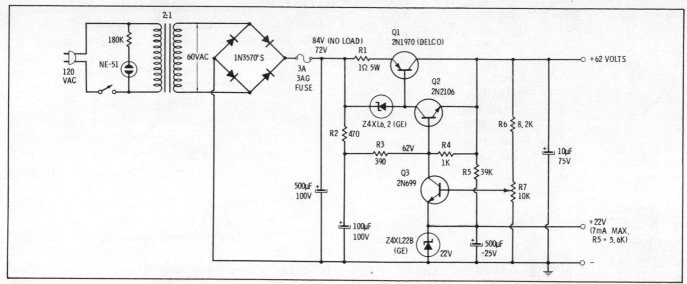

Fig. 9-13. Heavy-duty regulated power supply.

Courtesy General Electric Company

normal regulation characteristic of this power supply. It shows equal regulating ability for all load currents up to 350 mA, and 2 percent voltage regulation at 400 mA. At no load, the normal peak-to-peak ripple voltage is 0.01 volt, increasing to nearly 0.3 volt at 400 mA load current. Of course, if one or more of the filter capacitors should become defective, the ripple voltage would be much greater.

Most modern organs use somewhat more complex voltage-regulator circuits to obtain even closer regulation. The configuration shown in Fig. 9-13 utilizes a Darlington connection for the series regulating element (Q1 and Q2). A Darlington pair of transistors is characterized by very high gain. This regulated dc supply also features higher current capability than the arrangement in Fig. 9-12. It can supply up to 2 amperes, at an output voltage from 45 to 65 volts. The exact output voltage is determined by the setting of R7 in Fig. 9-13. In normal operation, the output ripple is less than 0.001 volt at no load, increasing to 0.06 volt at 2 amperes load

current. In case the output terminals are accidentally short circuited, the 3-A fuse will blow before component damage occurs. For example, if the 10-μF filter capacitor short-circuits, the fuse will blow.

Two output voltages are available in the arrangement of Fig. 9-13. The +22-volt output is regulated by the zener diode, and is rated for a maximum output current of 7 mA. If this output line is accidentally short circuited, the fuse will blow because of abnormally heavy transistor conduction. The same observation applies to the simpler configuration shown in Fig. 9-12. In any branched power supply, it is necessary to find out which branch is causing the overload before a fuse can be replaced. That is, if a replacement fuse blows immediately when it is inserted, we have the task of localizing the overloaded branch. This is most easily done by disconnection. For example, there are five branches to be considered in the configuration of Fig. 9-14, if we consider the possibility of fuse-blowing due to

Fig. 9-14. Power supply with branched outputs.

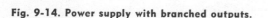
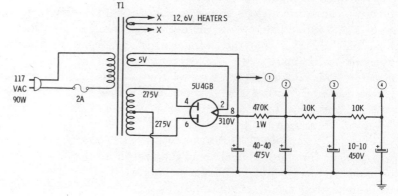

heater-circuit overload. If the branch lines are progressively disconnected, the overload path can be quickly determined. Then, resistance measurements in the associated circuit will usually serve to close in on the defective component.

Troubleshooting is facilitated in power-supply designs that provide a circuit breaker in each branch line, as in the example of Fig. 9-1. Five branch lines are used, with a circuit breaker for each. If one of the branches becomes overloaded, the associated breaker opens the circuit and gives a visual indication of trouble. Of course, the circuit breakers cannot protect the power supply against shorted rectifier diodes X1 through X4, or against shorts in the transformer windings, etc. However, the 5-ampere slow-blow fuse provides against overload damage from these sources. If the power demand reaches 600 watts, or more, the fuse will blow quickly. Note that a small organ might have a power supply that is fused to blow quickly at a power demand of 100 watts.

Apprentices should note that a fuse does not protect a circuit directly against excessive power consumption. A fuse provides indirect protection, because its operation is dependent upon current flow, and not upon power consumption. For example, a fuse that is rated to blow at 5 amperes provides the same current protection in either a 90-volt circuit or in a 120-volt circuit. In a 90-volt circuit, the fuse will blow when the power consumption is equal to 450 watts. On the other hand, in a 120-volt circuit, the same fuse will blow when the power consumption is equal to 600 watts. Therefore, a given fuse provides less protection against component damage when the line voltage is high. Although a fuse is rated for a certain voltage, this rating merely ensures that arc-over will not occur at the specified voltage when the fusible element opens. The same general observations apply to circuit breakers.

It is instructive also to note some basic facts concerning power factors. With reference to Fig. 9-15, a resistive load consumes real power when connected to an ac source. Real power is measured in watts; it is also called true power, or in-phase power. In-phase power means that the voltage drop across the resistor is in phase with the current through the resistor. The power factor of a resistive load is 100 percent. On the other hand, a capacitive load operates on the basis of reactive power when connected to an ac source, as shown in Fig. 9-15B. No power is actually consumed, because power is stored in the capacitor for one-half cycle, and then returned to the source during the next half-cycle. Reactive power is measured in vars (volt-amperes-reactive).

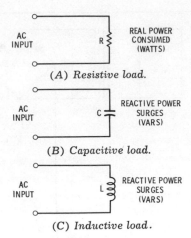

Fig. 9-15. Three basic power situations.

It is also called imaginary power, or quadrature power. The power factor of a capacitive load is 0 percent. The same general observations hold true for an inductive load, as shown in Fig. 9-15C. There is a distinction, however: in a capacitive load, the current leads the applied voltage by 90°, whereas in an inductive load, the current lags the applied voltage by 90°.

Next, let us consider the situations in which each of the loads in Fig. 9-15 has an ohmic value that draws 3 amperes from the source. If a 2-ampere fuse is inserted in each circuit, the fuses will blow in each case. In other words, the blowing point of a fuse has no relation to the power factor of the load. A fuse blows simply on the basis of current flow. Whether the power is real or imaginary makes no difference. Power supplies operate at a comparatively high power factor in normal operation. However, any power supply draws a little imaginary power, in addition to its real-power demand. A simple situation is shown in Fig. 9-16, in which the load is both resistive and capacitive. The resistor draws real power, and the capacitor operates on imaginary power. *A wattmeter connected to the input terminals of the power supply will read the real power only.*

Note that real power and imaginary power are related by an electrical unit called the volt-ampere, as illustrated in Fig. 9-17. Let us suppose that we measure the line voltage, and find that it is 117 volts. In turn, if the primary of a power-supply transformer draws 2 amperes, we should *not* state that the power consumption is 2 × 117 or 234 watts. That is, we have not measured the true power value, and

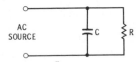

Fig. 9-16. A load that draws both real and imaginary power.

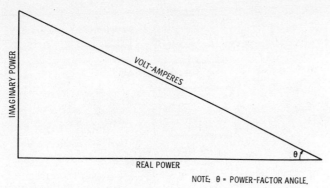

Fig. 9-17. Relation of real power and imaginary power to volt-amperes.

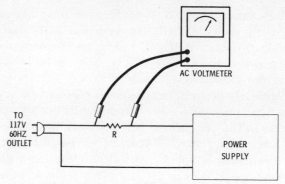

Fig. 9-19. Practical alternating current measurement.

the correct statement is that there are 234 volt-amperes in the primary. Next, if we connect a wattmeter to the primary terminals, we might measure a true-power value of 200 watts. In turn, the imaginary power is about 121 vars, as shown in Fig. 9-18.

The angle θ (theta) in Fig. 9-17 is called the power-factor angle. The power factor is defined as the cosine of theta. For example, let us suppose that an ac circuit draws 400 watts of real power, operates with an imaginary power of 300 watts, and therefore has a 500 volt-ampere value. In this example, the power-factor angle is 36° 52′, and the power factor is 0.800, or 80 percent. In other words, we can check the real power consumption with a wattmeter, but this measurement does not necessarily correspond to the current that is present.

To measure alternating current, it is usually most practical to use the test setup shown in Fig. 9-19. A suitable power resistor is connected in series with the power cord, and an ac voltmeter is connected across the resistor. A resistance value of 1 ohm is convenient, because each volt indicated on the meter scale then corresponds to a current of 1 ampere. The resistor must be rated for the necessary power dissipation (such as 300 watts), and should have a fairly close tolerance to ensure accurate measurements.

For example, 5-percent power resistors are readily available and are not unduly expensive. Remember that the resistor will run hot—if it is enclosed in a ventilated housing, you will not burn your fingers accidentally.

INTERFERENCE

When installing an electronic organ, it should be kept in mind that it is not customary to provide line filters in the power supplies, and that it is quite possible for line interference that enters the power supply to make objectionable "plunks" or rasping noises in the tones that are produced. Therefore, it is advisable that a separate circuit be used for service to the organ console. A 15-ampere circuit is adequate for all but the largest instruments. This precaution ensures that organ operation will be unaffected by switching of household appliances or other devices that draw appreciable current. Note that tone cabinets containing individual amplifiers with power supplies should also be operated from a separate 117-volt circuit. If it is desired to check a particular outlet for transients, a scope check can be made as indicated in Fig. 9-20. This test serves to distinguish between noises originating from the 117-volt supply line and noises that may be produced by malfunctioning devices or components in the organ circuitry.

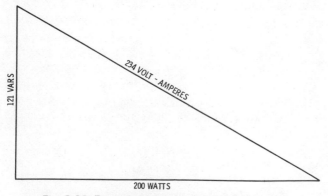

Fig. 9-18. Example of a load drawing substantial imaginary power.

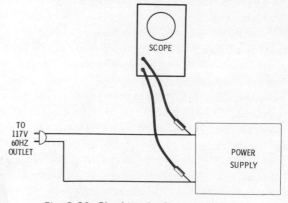

Fig. 9-20. Checking for line interference.

Glossary

Accompaniment. Also called *lower* or *Great.* The lower manual of an organ, which provides the musical harmony to the solo or melody.

Action. An organ action denotes the assembly of key contacts and couplers.

Aeolian. A very soft organ stop of mild string quality.

Amplifier. The section of an electronic organ that increases the amplitude of tone-signal waveforms.

Amplitude. Also called *peak value.* The maximum value of a waveform, subclassified into positive and negative peak values.

Anode. The electrode at which electrons leave a device to enter the external circuit.

Attack. (Related to *rise time.*) The period of time during which a tone increases to full intensity after the key has been depressed.

Arpeggio. Playing the notes of a chord in rapid sequence, instead of simultaneously. Sometimes accomplished by automatic circuit action.

Autotransformer. A transformer designed with a single, tapped winding, which serves as both primary and secondary.

Baffle. A partition or enclosure in a tone cabinet that increases the length of the air path from the front to the rear radiating surfaces of the speaker.

Baroque. Baroque music is a basic form of composition characterized by ornamentation and powerful climaxes.

Bass. The lower or pedal tones provided by an organ.

Bass-Reflex Enclosure. A tone-cabinet enclosure in which a portion of the radiation from the rear of the speaker is used to reinforce the bass tones.

Beat. Denotes a successive rising and falling of a wave envelope due to alternate reinforcements and cancellations of two or more component frequencies.

Bourdon. Denotes a low-pitched wood-flute organ pipe.

Brass. A generalized term denoting tones resembling those from brass instruments such as the tuba, trumpet, or cornet.

Bridge. A precision electrical instrument for the measurement of resistance, capacitance, and inductance values.

Buffer. A device, such as a tube or transistor, employed between an ac source and its load, principally for purposes of isolation.

Bus Bar. A bare electrical conductor that connects to various tone sources, or that distributes voltages to various points in an organ system.

Capacitor. (Obs: *Condenser.*) Any device designed for storage of electrostatic field energy.

Carillon. A bell tower actuated from a keyboard. In an electronic organ, the tones may be generated electronically.

Celeste. A stop characterized by a slow beat of 3 or 4 Hz. It is used in the upper register, usually in the diapason family.

Cent. An interval between two tones, with a value of approximately 1/100 semitone.

Chimes. A bell-like tone produced by striking metal tubes or rods with a hammer, or by equivalent electronic synthesis.

Choir. An organ voice produced by blending several tones (of the same family) that have practically the same pitch, but differing phases. Sometimes, the choir effect is simulated by blending several tones with a phase difference produced by frequency-modulating one or more of the tones.

Chord. A combination of harmonious tones that are sounded simultaneously.

Chord Coupling. A coupling mode in which all tones for a specific chord can be played by depressing a single button or key.

Chord Organ. An organ arranged for playing a variety of chords in harmony with solo tones. Each chord is played by depressing a single button or key.

Chorus Effect. Same as *choir*, q.v.

Chromatic Keyboard. A keyboard with the black notes placed at the same height as the white notes, and with the same widths, to facilitate playing of chromatic scales.

Chromatic Scale. A scale composed entirely of half-steps.

Chromatic Percussion. Percussive effects that are applied to notes of the organ, to simulate struck strings, plucked strings, marimba, or xylophone voices.

Cipher. A tone that is produced when no key is depressed.

Clarinet. An organ stop for a voice that simulates clarinet tones.

Clavier. Any keyboard or pedalboard operated with either the hands or the feet. A hand-operated clavier is more often called a *manual.*

Complex Tone. An audio waveform composed of a fundamental frequency and a number of integrally related harmonic frequencies (a pitch and a number of integrally related overtones).

Concordant. A series of musically meaningful tones.

Console. The cabinet that houses an organ.

Contra. When prefixed to the name of a musical instrument, this term signifies that the tones have been lowered one octave.

Cornopean. An organ voice with a rich and horn-like tone color.

Counterbass. Also termed *contrabass,* signifying a second bass note that will harmonize with a particular chord.

Coupler. A stop tablet that permits the tones on one manual to be played with the keys of another manual, or that permits the sounding of octavely related tones on the same manual.

Crescendo. A pedal or equivalent control in an organ that rapidly brings all stops into play; an increase in voice output to maximum power capability.

Crossover Network. A pair of filters that distribute the output audio energy into two channels according to frequency range, for application to indi-

vidual woofer and tweeter speakers. Three distribution channels may be used in elaborate systems.

Cymbal. A high-pitched mixture stop that simulates the metallic clashing sound of orchestra cymbals.

Decay. The period of time over which a tone decreases from peak volume to inaudibility. Technically, the basic exponential function defines the natural law of decay (and growth).

Decibel. (dB.) A unit of measurement for change in sound level or amplitude of an audio signal. One decibel is equal to one-tenth of a bel, and is about the smallest change that can be detected by a listener.

Delay Line. An electromechanical transmission line (or equivalent) for delaying a signal or impulse in passage between the input and output terminals; often terminated in comparatively high or low impedances, to obtain energy reflections (reverberation).

Diapason. The basic tone color of traditional organ voices, as produced by open or stopped pipes.

Discordant. Tones that are unrelated by established principles of harmony.

Diode. A unilateral electronic device used in rectification, waveshaping, switching, and other applications.

Divider. A circuit, device, or arrangement that reduces a voltage or signal to a certain fraction of its input value, or that generates a subharmonic of an input signal frequency.

Dividing Network. Same as *Crossover Network,* q.v.

Doppler Tone Cabinet. A tone-cabinet design in which one or more speakers are rotated or in which a baffle is rotated to obtain a mechanical vibrato effect.

Double Touch. A key-contact design that provides actuation of an additional circuit when somewhat more than normal finger pressure is applied.

Drawbar. An arrangement for combining tones in voicing systems; a drawbar is pushed in and pulled out, instead of being pressed as a stop tab.

Dulciana. A flute voice with a small and slightly stringy tone.

Eccles-Jordan Oscillator. Also termed a flip-flop, or a bistable multivibrator; used chiefly for frequency division.

Expression Control. An organ volume control, usually operated with the right foot.

Extended Octave. A tone above or below a note on a standard keyboard that sounds when a specific coupler is actuated.

Fast Decay. Rapid attenuation of a tone after the keyswitch is released.

FET. (Field-effect transistor.) A transistor of the voltage-operated device classification, rather than current-operated.

Filter Network. A reactive network designed to provide specified attenuation to signals within certain frequency limits. Basic filters are termed low-pass, high-pass, and bandpass types.

Flat. A note a half-step or semitone lower than its related natural pitch.

Flute. The one of the four basic tone colors that simulates the orchestral flute; it has the most nearly sinusoidal waveform of the four basic tone colors.

Formant Filter. A waveshaping network or device that changes the waveform of a tone-generator signal into a desired tonal waveform.

Forte. A forte tab (solo tab) increases the volume of other tabs that are depressed at the time; a forte tab has no voice of its own.

Foundation Voice. A definitive organ voice, such as the diapason and dulciana voices.

Free-Running Oscillator. An oscillator that generates an output in the absence of a synchronizing signal or trigger signal, as opposed to an Eccles-Jordan oscillator, q.v.

Frequency. The number of complete vibrations or cycles completed in one second by a waveform, and measured in Hertz.

Frequency Range. Limiting values of a frequency spectrum, such as 20 Hz to 20 kHz.

Frequency Response. The frequency range over which an audio device or system will produce or reproduce a signal within a certain tolerance, such as ±1 dB.

Fundamental. The normal pitch of a musical tone; usually, the lowest frequency component of a tonal waveform.

Gate Circuit. A circuit that operates as a selective switch and permits conduction over a specified interval.

Gemshorn. A flute organ voice with a bright tone color.

Generator. A tone source, such as an oscillator, frequency divider, magnetic tone wheel, etc.

Glide. Also termed *Glissando*. A rapid series of tones, produced by a slight shift in pitch on successive tones.

Glockenspiel. Also called *Orchestra Bells*. An electromechanical arrangement that simulates the bells used in orchestras.

Great Manual. Also called *accompaniment manual*, or *lower manual*. The keyboard used for playing the accompaniment to a melody.

Half-Tone. Also termed *Semitone*. The relation between adjacent pitches on the tempered scale.

Harmonic. A frequency component of a complex waveform that bears an integral relation to the fundamental frequency. Also called an *Overtone*.

Harmony. Musical support for a melody, consisting of two or more notes played simultaneously.

IC. Abbreviation for *Integrated Circuit*. Integral solid-state units that include transistors, resistors, semiconductor diodes, and often capacitors, which are formed simultaneously during fabrication.

Interval. The difference in pitch between two musical tones.

Keybed. A shelf or horizontal surface on which the keyboard is mounted.

Keyboard. A bank of keys, comprising white and black sets, arranged in ascending tones.

Keynote. The tonic, or first note of a given scale.

Keyswitch. A switch that closes when a key is depressed, thereby actuating a tone generator.

Kinura. A reed stop that has dominant harmonics and a subordinate fundamental.

Leslie Speaker. A generic term, originally a trade name, denoting a tone cabinet with a mechanical vibrato assembly.

Manual. Also termed a *Clavier*, q.v.

Master Oscillator. The source of a tone signal; it may be employed directly, or processed through one or more frequency dividers; the latter are also oscillators, but of the synchronized or driven type.

Mechanicals. Denote organ effects that are not voices in the strict sense of the term; includes forte (solo) and percussion effects and couplers.

Mechanical Tone Generator. A mechanical device for the generation of electrical impulses that are subsequently converted into audible tones.

Megohm. A multiple unit denoting one million ohms.

Melodia. A solo stop of the flute family.

Melody. Often called a tune in a musical composition; usually played sequentially note-by-note on the swell or solo manual.

Modulation. A process whereby low-frequency information is encoded into a higher frequency (sometimes called the carrier). The three modulating processes used in electronic organs are called amplitude, frequency, and phase modulation.

Multivibrator. A relaxation oscillator, usually developing a semisquare wave output. Multivibrators are subclassified into free-running (astable), monostable, and bistable types.

Muting. A silencing process or action.

Nazard. A voice simulating a piccolo-type organ pipe.

Neon Lamp. A gas diode, used as a pilot lamp or indicator lamp, and occasionally as a relaxation-oscillator device. Sometimes used also as a frequency-divider device, or switching device.

Nonchromatic Percussion. A percussion effect that has no dominant pitch, such as wood-block, drum, castanet, and cymbal sounds.

Note. A single musical tone, identified by letters of the alphabet from A through G, plus sharp or flat superscripts.

Octave. A pair of tones are said to be separated by an octave if one of the tones has twice the frequency of the other.

Octave Coupling. A coupling arrangement in which the depression of a key causes a note one octave higher (or lower) to sound simultaneously.

Oscillator. An electronic, electrical, or electromechanical generator of an electrical signal that corresponds to a note on the musical scale.

Outphasing. A method of voicing wherein specified harmonics or subharmonics are added to or subtracted from a tone-generator signal prior to its application to a formant filter. In *Chiff* circuits, certain harmonics are added, but only during the attack period.

Overtone. Same as *Harmonic*, q.v.

Partial. Any one of the various frequencies contained in a complex waveform that corresponds to a musical tone.

Pedal. The pedal keyboard of an organ; also called *Clavier*, q.v.

Pedal Clavier. A pedal keyboard.

Pedal Divider. The frequency-divider section associated with the tone generators actuated by the foot pedals.

Pedal Generator. A tone generator used to produce the bass notes of an organ.

Pedal Board. Same as *Pedal Clavier*, q.v.

Pedal Keyboard. Same as *Pedal Clavier*, q.v.

Percussion. Characteristic tones, such as produced by plucking or striking strings.

pF. Abb. for *picofarad*.

Phase Inverter. An amplifier that provides an output 180° out of phase with the input, or one that provides a pair of outputs that are 180° out of phase with each other.

Phase-Shift Oscillator. An oscillator that obtains its own input from a 180° phase-shifting network connected between its input and output terminals.

Picofarad. One micro-microfarad.

Piston. A stop that is operated by pushing or pulling a knob. A piston usually operates groups of conventional stops.

Pitch. The characteristic of a sound which places it on a musical scale.

Pizzicato. A sound effect that simulates the rapid plucking of strings.

Power. The rate of doing work, measured in watt units. May refer to the power consumption of an organ, or to its audio power output.

Power Supply. The section of an organ that supplies electrical power for operation of the various circuits.

Preset. A control that turns a group of voices on or off without actuating any tabs.

Pulse. An electrical transient, or a series of repetitive surges.

Quality. The harmonic content of a tone that corresponds to the musical characteristic termed *Timbre*, q.v.

Reed. The one of the four basic tone-color groups of voices that simulates orchestral reeds.

Register. The range of notes included by a clavier or manual; the range of notes employed in playing a particular musical composition.

Relay. An electromagnetically operated switching device that actuates one or many contacts.

Resultant. Denotes a tone produced when two notes a fifth apart and an octave higher than the desired note are sounded to produce the desired pitch. A mode of producing *Synthetic Bass*, q.v.

Reverberation. Persistence of sound due to echoes, either natural or artificial.

Rhythm Section. An organ section that generates nonchromatic percussion effects in a periodic manner, either automatically or manually.

Scale. A series of eight consecutive whole notes.

Semitone. The relation between adjacent pitches on the tempered scale.

Sforzando. A form of *Crescendo* (q.v.), but employing discordant tones also.

Sharp. A note removed by a semitone in pitch from the reference note.

Sine Wave. Simple harmonic motion represented graphically.

Solo Manual. Upper manual of a two-manual organ, generally used for playing the melody. Also called the *Swell Manual.*

Speaker. A transducer that converts electrical energy into sound energy.

Standing Waves. Reflected waves that cancel and reinforce one another at various locations within an enclosed space.

Stops. A tab or other form of switch that selects and/or mixes the various voices and footages in an electronic organ.

String. The one of the four basic tone-color groups that simulates orchestral strings.

Sustain. An effect that is produced by a note that diminishes gradually in its intensity after the key has been released.

Subharmonic. An integral submultiple of the fundamental frequency of the sound to which it is related.

Swell Manual. Upper manual of an organ; also called the *Solo Manual.*

Synthetic Bass. A mode of bass-tone generation that exploits the nonlinear characteristic of the ear. The pertinent harmonics are produced, but the fundamental is omitted; in turn, the ear generates the omitted fundamental as a subharmonic of the incomplete waveform.

Tablet. (*Abb. Tab.*) Rocker-type switch control that selects a voice or a footage.

Temperament. Denotes a mode of tuning an instrument scale so that successive tones correspond to specified intervals.

Tempered Scale. Arrangement of musical pitches so that successive notes have equal frequency ratios.

Tibia. An organ voice that simulates flute tones, although not precisely.

Timbre. (Also termed *Tone Color.*) It is the distinguishing quality of a sound, which depends primarily upon the harmonic structure of its waveform. However, timbre also depends upon the volume level of the reproduced sound.

Tone. Denotes the fundamental sound of a musical note.

Tone Color. (Same as *Timbre,* q.v.) The four chief tone colors of an electronic organ are *Diapason, Flute, String,* and *Reed,* q.v.

Tone Generator. A section of an organ that generates the original electrical waveforms that are subsequently processed into voices and radiated from the tone cabinet(s).

Tone Wheel. A rotating disc-shaped armature used in mechanical tone generators.

Toy Counter. Denotes a section of an organ that produces nonchromatic and special-effects or comparatively novel voice modifications.

Transient. An electrical surge. A succession of transients at uniform intervals is usually termed a *Pulse Waveform.*

Transistor. Generic name for a family of semiconductor devices having at least three electrodes, and providing amplifier action primarily, although not exclusively.

Tremolo. Technically, an amplitude modulation of a tone at a rate of approximately seven hertz.

Tuning Fork. A precision mechanically resonant device used as a frequency reference. Usually fabricated in the basic horseshoe shape, but sometimes designed as a rectangular or round bar, supported at its nodal points.

Varistor. A voltage-dependent resistor.

Vibrato. Technically, a frequency modulation of a tone at a rate of approximately seven hertz. A *Doppler Tone Cabinet* (q.v.) employs both vibrato and tremolo effects.

Voice. The resultant tone output obtained through the mixing of various harmonics to imitate a musical instrument or other effect.

Voicing Tab. Same as *Tablet,* q.v.

Volume. Denotes a sound level; usually termed *Expression* in organ context.

Watt. The unit of power. It is equal to the product of current and voltage.

Wow-Wow. A very slow vibrato provided by some modern organs.

FREQUENCIES OF THE TEMPERED SCALE
(Frequencies in Hertz)

C	C#	D	D#
16.35	17.32	18.35	19.44
32.70	34.65	36.71	38.89
65.41	69.30	73.42	77.78
130.81	138.59	146.83	155.56
261.62	277.18	293.66	311.13
523.25	554.36	587.33	622.25
1046.50	1108.73	1174.66	1244.51
2093.00	2217.46	2349.32	2489.01
4186.01	4434.92	4698.64	4978.03
8372.02	8869.84	9397.27	9956.06
16744.03			

E	F	F#	G
20.60	21.83	23.12	24.50
41.20	43.65	46.25	49.00
82.41	87.31	92.50	98.00
164.81	174.61	185.00	196.00
329.63	349.23	369.99	392.00
659.26	698.46	739.99	783.99
1318.51	1396.91	1479.98	1567.98
2637.02	2793.82	2959.95	3135.96
5274.04	5587.65	5919.90	6270.93
10548.08	11157.30	11839.81	12541.86

G#	A	A#	B
25.96	27.50	29.14	30.87
51.91	55.00	58.27	61.74
103.83	110.00	116.54	123.47
207.65	220.00	233.08	246.94
415.30	440.00	466.16	493.88
830.61	880.00	932.33	987.77
1661.22	1760.00	1864.65	1975.53
3322.44	3520.00	3729.31	3951.06
6644.87	7040.00	7458.62	7902.13
13289.74	14080.00	14917.23	15804.26

CCCC 16.35 Hz is the lowest note of 32 ft pitch.
CCC 32.70 Hz is the lowest note of 16 ft pitch.
CC 65.41 Hz is the lowest note of 8 ft pitch.
C 261.62 Hz is the popularly termed middle C of the keyboard.

ELECTRONIC SYMBOLS

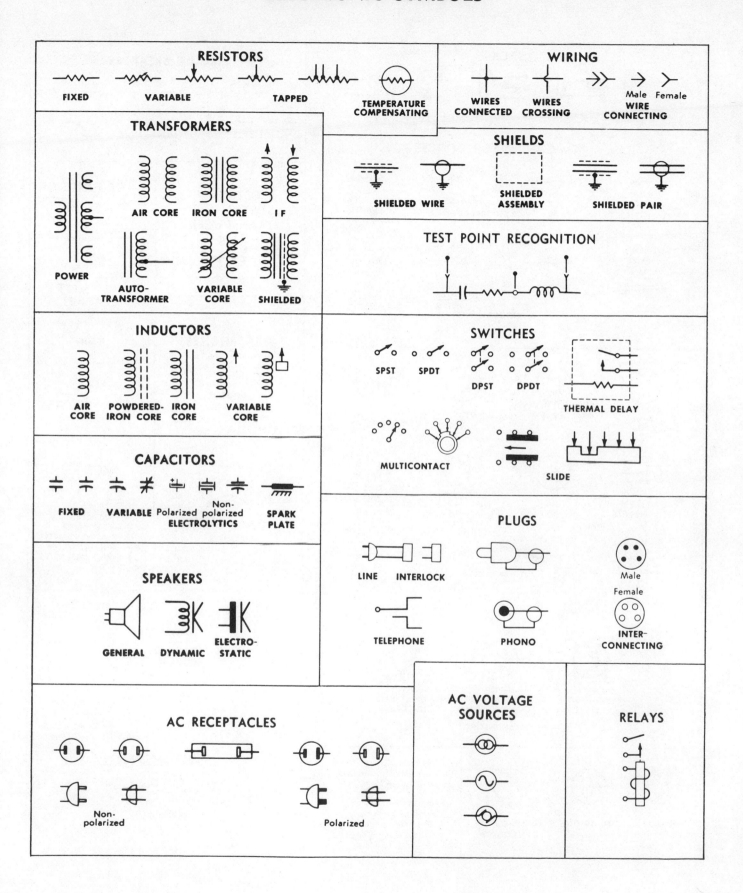

RESISTORS
FIXED   VARIABLE   TAPPED   TEMPERATURE COMPENSATING

WIRING
WIRES CONNECTED   WIRES CROSSING   Male   Female   WIRE CONNECTING

TRANSFORMERS
AIR CORE   IRON CORE   I F
POWER   AUTO-TRANSFORMER   VARIABLE CORE   SHIELDED

SHIELDS
SHIELDED WIRE   SHIELDED ASSEMBLY   SHIELDED PAIR

TEST POINT RECOGNITION

INDUCTORS
AIR CORE   POWDERED-IRON CORE   IRON CORE   VARIABLE CORE

SWITCHES
SPST   SPDT   DPST   DPDT   THERMAL DELAY
MULTICONTACT   SLIDE

CAPACITORS
FIXED   VARIABLE   Polarized   Non-polarized   SPARK PLATE
ELECTROLYTICS

SPEAKERS
GENERAL   DYNAMIC   ELECTRO-STATIC

PLUGS
LINE   INTERLOCK   Male
TELEPHONE   PHONO   Female   INTER-CONNECTING

AC RECEPTACLES
Non-polarized   Polarized

AC VOLTAGE SOURCES

RELAYS

ELECTRONIC SYMBOLS

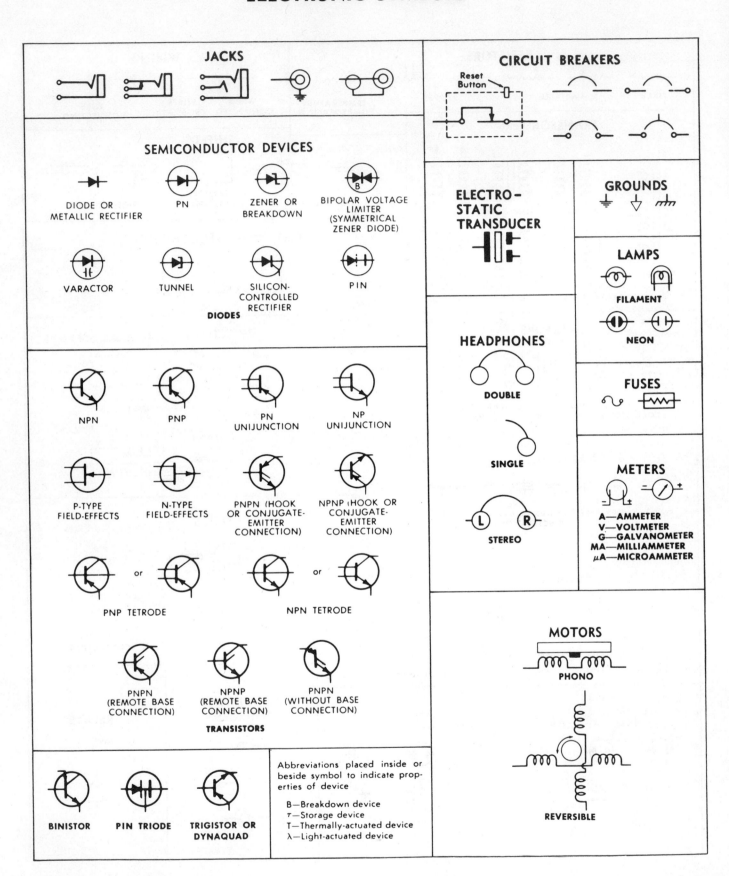

JACKS

CIRCUIT BREAKERS

Reset Button

SEMICONDUCTOR DEVICES

DIODE OR METALLIC RECTIFIER

PN

ZENER OR BREAKDOWN

BIPOLAR VOLTAGE LIMITER (SYMMETRICAL ZENER DIODE)

VARACTOR

TUNNEL

SILICON-CONTROLLED RECTIFIER

PIN

DIODES

NPN

PNP

PN UNIJUNCTION

NP UNIJUNCTION

P-TYPE FIELD-EFFECTS

N-TYPE FIELD-EFFECTS

PNPN (HOOK OR CONJUGATE-EMITTER CONNECTION)

NPNP (HOOK OR CONJUGATE-EMITTER CONNECTION)

or

or

PNP TETRODE

NPN TETRODE

PNPN (REMOTE BASE CONNECTION)

NPNP (REMOTE BASE CONNECTION)

PNPN (WITHOUT BASE CONNECTION)

TRANSISTORS

BINISTOR

PIN TRIODE

TRIGISTOR OR DYNAQUAD

Abbreviations placed inside or beside symbol to indicate properties of device

B—Breakdown device
τ—Storage device
T—Thermally-actuated device
λ—Light-actuated device

ELECTRO-STATIC TRANSDUCER

HEADPHONES

DOUBLE

SINGLE

L R

STEREO

GROUNDS

LAMPS

FILAMENT

NEON

FUSES

METERS

A—AMMETER
V—VOLTMETER
G—GALVANOMETER
MA—MILLIAMMETER
μA—MICROAMMETER

MOTORS

PHONO

REVERSIBLE

Index